QUIN
RID
BIR

The Work of
ROBERT ADAM

The illustration reproduced overleaf is the frontispiece from Robert Adam's folio *Ruins of the Palace of the Emperor Diocletian, at Spalatro, in Dalmatia* (1764). The plates in the volume were engraved in Venice under the supervision of Clérisseau and James Adam; Robert had undertaken the hectic survey of the palace in 1757. (Photograph: Manchester University, John Rylands Library.)

IMPERATORIS
DIOCLETIANI PALATII
RVINAE
PROPE SALONAM.

The Work of
ROBERT ADAM

Geoffrey Beard

John Bartholomew & Son Limited
Edinburgh and London

British Library Cataloguing in Publication Data
Beard, Geoffrey
  The work of Robert Adam.
  1. Adam, Robert
  I. Title
  720'.92'4   NA997.A4

  ISBN 0-7028-1087-8

First published in Great Britain 1978 by
JOHN BARTHOLOMEW & SON LIMITED
12 Duncan Street, Edinburgh EH9 1TA
And 216 High Street, Bromley BR1 1PW

Second impression 1978

ISBN 0 7028 1087 8

Book and jacket design: Susan Waywell
11/12 pt, 12/13 pt Monophoto Bembo (270)

Colour reproduction by Kleur Litho Ltd,
Bexleyheath, Kent

Printed in Great Britain by
Hazell Watson & Viney Ltd, Aylesbury, Bucks

CONTENTS

PREFACE

This book is being published 250 years after the birth, in Scotland in 1728, of the architect Robert Adam. It is intended as a record and analysis of the contribution Robert made to eighteenth-century architecture and decoration, and less attention is therefore paid to biographical details.

The Adam style blended together a great variety of motifs from many sources – Roman, Greek, Etruscan, and Palladian among them – with sideways looks at interpretations by Bartoli, Piranesi, William Kent, and others. A. T. Bolton, to whose two-volume work of 1922 on the Adam brothers all following students are much indebted, described it thus: 'Robert Adam came at the ebb and flow, between the lapsing classic and the rising romantic movements and having by temperament sympathies alive to the influence of both, his work in its results was bound to exhibit their opposing characteristics'. It was flexible, it allowed compromise, and was executed with care by firm direction of 'a regiment of artificers'. It succeeded in transforming from the late 1750s onwards many English, Scottish, and, by transference through individuals and pattern-books, some American, Russian, and Irish interiors.

This book is intended for readers interested in eighteenth-century architecture and decoration, and attention is therefore drawn to an extensive specialized literature. The researches of, in particular, John Fleming, Nicholas Goodison, John and Eileen Harris, Professor Alistair Rowan, and Dr Damie Stillman have established important facts about Adam's life and work. They have kindly corresponded and worked with me on these and related studies over many years.

In the brief introductory essay that follows I have tried to take note of such researches so that they help to a better understanding of the colour and monochrome illustrations, which are divided into three main sections: a small group of portraits of Robert and his family; reproductions of drawings made by him, or under his direction, both on his Italian tour and for the later major commissions; general views and details of most of the completed and extant works, ranging from grand conceptions such as the south front of Kedleston, and the richly decorated interiors at Syon and Osterley, to the minute detailing of such objects as door furnishings, mirrors, tables, chimneypieces, chairs, silver, and carpets. The plates are accompanied by what Robert and James Adam in their own splendid folio the *Works in Architecture* (1773–8) called 'a short explanation . . . with such observations as we imagined might be both useful and entertaining'.

In compiling this book I am much indebted to those who have helped me to gather suitable illustrations. First among these is the distinguished architectural photographer A. F. Kersting, F.R.P.S., who has provided almost a half of the total, including new views of Syon; Osterley; 20 St James's Square, London;

PREFACE

Culzean; Harewood; Mellerstain; Newby; and Nostell. They have been taken with the ready cooperation of the Duke of Northumberland; the Victoria & Albert Museum; the Distillers' Company; the National Trust for Scotland; the Earl of Harewood; the Viscount Binning; Mr and Mrs Robin Compton; and Lord St Oswald. In addition Maurice Tomlin, John Hardy, and Martha Gerson of the Department of Furniture and Woodwork, Victoria & Albert Museum, allowed me the use of the very detailed study of Osterley they had undertaken. This has enabled me to select about twenty previously unpublished photographs of details of ornament at that important house.

Drawings, portraits, and other relevant works have been reproduced by courtesy of the Trustees of Sir John Soane's Museum; Mr Keith Adam; Sir John Clerk, Bt; Cumbria County Record Office; Laing Art Gallery, Newcastle upon Tyne; the Yale Center for British Art, Yale University; the National Portrait Gallery; the Scottish National Portrait Gallery; and Mr Jocelyn E. B. Stevens. The source of all such material and of the photographs is given in the 'Notes on the Plates'.

Many friends helped in the obtaining of suitable photographs – an acknowledgment of their names is necessary but hardly adequate as recognition of their work on my behalf. They include Catherine Cruft (Scottish National Monuments Record); John Kerslake (National Portrait Gallery); David Learmont (National Trust for Scotland); Dr Duncan Thomson (Scottish National Portrait Gallery); David DuBon (Philadelphia Museum of Art); Charles Hammond (Gore Place, Waltham, Massachusetts), and Morrison H. Heckscher (Metropolitan Museum of Art, New York).

For their help with other aspects of research or publication I acknowledge the care and consideration shown by Trevor Chriss; George Clarke; Michael Felmingham; Judith Goodison; G. H. Roberton; Robert Rowe; Christine Scull; Gaye Smith; Joe Thomson; Stephen Yates; and finally my wife and daughter, who have stepped around piles of photographs for too many months with a fortitude born of experience, a concern for Robert Adam, and for me.

Geoffrey Beard
University of Lancaster
October 1977

INTRODUCTION

I

RUINS, VILLAS, AND PALACES

The English patron's enthusiasm for building and embellishing great country houses, especially in the eighteenth century, not only demanded large financial resources but also provided an opportunity for new decorative styles to evolve and gain acceptance. The architects and craftsmen employed during this period possessed both abundant energy and a wide variety of talents, and they produced schemes of building and decoration that were both diverse and accomplished. These ranged from the classically proportioned columns and porticoes of Palladianism and the exuberant swirling forms of the Rococo to the mannered elegance of the Gothic and Chinese styles. The last half of the century encompassed the ordered symmetry of Neo-Classicism. This new mood was given a significant and influential direction by the efforts in particular of the architect Robert Adam (pls. 1, 5), born at Kirkcaldy in Scotland on 3 July 1728. The style he championed for his major works was fused into a personal statement that based itself on his early Scottish training – his father (pl. 2) was the first strictly classical architect that Scotland produced – his Grand Tour of Italy, and his extensive studies in Rome.

The earliest of these important architectural movements in eighteenth-century England sought to perpetuate the ideas of the sixteenth-century Italian master Andrea Palladio. His buildings and plans had been sought out early in the seventeenth century when the English classical architect Inigo Jones (1573–1652) was travelling in Italy in the entourage of Thomas, Earl of Arundel. The revived interest in the reign of George I owed its origin to two important source books, and to an influential set of Whig patrons. In 1715 Colen Campbell's first volume of drawings and plans, titled *Vitruvius Britannicus*, appeared, and in 1715–16 Giacomo Leoni, a Venetian architect newly arrived in England from service with the Elector Palatine, issued a two-volume edition of Palladio. Through his translator, the French architect Nicholas Dubois, who had come to England in the late seventeenth century, Leoni boldly claimed that after 'several years in preparing the Designs . . . there has been no Book hitherto more beautifully printed in England'. These folios, with their extravagant fulsome dedications, stimulated patrons such as the Duke of Argyll and the Earls of Burlington and Pembroke to develop their own flair for architectural matters. The result, added to the important work by both Campbell and Leoni, was a small group of great houses (Mereworth and Houghton are two examples). They were erected with a correct observance of the principles of Vitruvius and Palladio and the interpretations of Inigo Jones and Burlington's 'Il Signior', the architect and decorator William Kent (c. 1685–1748). In the construction of these buildings imagination was allowed little room.

While the Rococo, Gothic, and Chinese styles, which followed and overlapped each other in the 1740s and 1750s, were divergent from their sources, they had much in common with each other. They did not conform to simplicity or regular pattern, and decorative elements, often wild and exuberant, adorn them all. Even the drawings of severe Palladian doorways made in the 1740s by the London architect Isaac Ware – who had dedicated his 1738 translation of Palladio, more precise and scholarly than Leoni's, to his patron, the Earl of Burlington – have Rococo foliage incorporated in them because, Ware argued, this was an allowable use of imagination. Chinese-style temples, furniture, and silver were loaded with mandarins and pagoda roofs. Lavish ornamentation became the leading feature of these middle years of a century that in its Palladian expression was looking for classical origins, in its Gothic back to a revered medieval past, and in Rococo to a world of present fantasy, the sprite-like touch of which was to enhance for a time even Gothic itself.

In the amazing super-abundance of taste that prevailed few could discern what taste really was. Nevertheless, helped along by a plentiful supply of French-inspired engravings after masters such as Meissonier, Pineau, and Cuvillies, it was a common striving to produce objects in carved wood to which the word could decently be applied. Some of the drawings showed settings that allowed complete escape into gay and frivolous dream-worlds. It was easy to forget what had been underlined so effectively in earlier years in the handsome pages of Palladio, 'that the very end of all buildings was to have some relation of one proportion to another, of the thing supporting to the thing supported, of the accessory to the principal, and of the parts to the whole'.

In the years leading up to 1750 society was highly sensitive to the venomous caricatures drawn by William Hogarth and was still unsettled by the sharp satires that had come from Swift and Pope. In such an atmosphere a host of more minor figures found their mark; James Cawthorn, for example (who constructed his poem *Of Taste* in 1756 on the basis that no one showed any common sense in contemporary architecture), inveighed in the periodicals about the absurdities of contemporary decoration. William Whitehead, indefatigable as a writer and complainer, wrote to the fashionable magazine *The World* in 1750 that 'the vases, busts and statues brought from Italy are flung into the garret to make room for great bellied Chinese pagods . . . whimsical buildings and temples that seem to be dedicated to no other deities than the winds'. This of course was an impetuous half-truth caused in part by the very character of lightness and grace of Chinoiserie, which eschewed the heavy scholastic approach of the Palladians.

Rococo was a more elusive style, but made an important if shortlived contribution to English interior decoration. Mirror and overmantel, engraved or in gilded wood, might appear to be submerged in the ebb and flow of decorative movements, but the basic structure was sound enough. English eyes became accustomed to the irregularities of the S and C scrolls with their perfect sense of balance and tension, and to being led 'a wanton kind of chace' in pursuit of decorative motifs. The gradual amelioration of the rules by such important and accurate a 'Burlingtonian' as Isaac Ware created in England a 'middle style' that was widely accepted and was a lasting influence on all forms of decoration.

The 'correction' of taste, which many felt was long overdue, slowly started when Robert Wood's books on the ruins of Palmyra and Baalbek appeared in 1753 and 1757. A writer in the *Monthly Review* wrote that he hoped Wood's informed volume on Baalbek might 'improve the taste of our countrymen and expel the littleness and ugliness of the Chinese, and the barbarity of the Goths that we may see no more useless and expensive trifles'. There was much that a sharp turn to Neo-Classicism could offer, and although patrons were ready to assume that it was something alien and foreign, it had firm roots in an established English system. There was already the classical building tradition, which Lord Burlington and his informed circle had given new impetus to by their acceptance of the work of the classical Roman architect Vitruvius, and the later work of Palladio. And since 1732 there had been in existence 'an association of gentlemen distinguished for their knowledge and taste in matters connected with the literature and antiquities of Greece and Italy' – banded together as 'The Society of Dilettanti' – who helped to promote a taste for classical art by sponsoring travel to, and books about, the classical antiquities in Greece and the Levant. Their sponsorship aided the travels of Robert Wood and publication of his discerning books on Palmyra and Baalbek, and the important publication in 1762 of Volume I of James Stuart's and Nicholas Revett's *Antiquities of Athens*. This enthusiasm for the classical world was generally shared by those fortunate enough to have had first-hand experience of it when on their Grand Tours; and this was important to James 'Athenian' Stuart, William Chambers, and Robert Adam when they returned home from long periods of study – Robert was in Italy from 1754 to 1758 – at the many classical sites and seats of learning, such as the French Academy in Rome, with a fresh yearning to emulate what had been seen. Since the mid century (from 1757) *Le Antichità di Ercolano* had appeared at intervals describing the recent discoveries at Pompeii, and Adam himself had spent several busy weeks with draughtsmen overseeing and surveying the ruins of Diocletian's Palace at Spalato. It was Robert Adam who now became the leader and vigorous exponent of a classical revival in England in architecture and decoration. He set the seal on what he had seen and knew to be a popular subject when he published his great volume on Diocletian's Palace in 1764 and presented a specially bound copy (col. pl. 1) to George III.

Robert Adam's first interests had centred in the late 1740s on the romantic and picturesque aspects of landscape, and Gothic buildings. His surviving Gothic sketches in a notebook at Blairadam (pls. 11–13) were the result of a great concern for Gothic detailing – one of his early drawings on his English tour in 1749 was of the Cross at Winchester. There was to come a time when elements of the Gothic would find their way into Adam's work as a variation to the classical, but at this early stage his drawings, inspired by a blend of observation and book searching (Batty Langley's *Gothic Architecture Improved* of 1742 was well thumbed by many besides Robert Adam and his brother James), show little trace of such eclecticism.

According to John Clerk of Eldin, who had married Robert's sister Susan, and who acted as a chronicler of much the architect did, it was on the English tour that 'he [Adam] first began to curb the exuberance of his fancy and polish his taste'. The skill in watercolouring he had refined in idle moments at the Ordnance commission of Fort George (pls. 29–30) on the Moray Firth, and by advice from the skilled watercolourist Paul Sandby, was soon to be put to a more exacting test under Italian skies. There were plenty of ancient ruins, Baroque churches, villas in the Alban Hills, and palaces of the Renaissance to suggest again the movement and reticulation of surface. All of them could be drawn, and travelling in the entourage of Charles Hope, brother of Lord Hopetoun, who had patronized his father, brother, and himself at his Scottish house (pls. 21–8), there were distinct social advantages and ease in arranging suitable introductions. They left for Italy in late October 1754, and the young architect had already grasped that such patronage could be a means to success: Lord Hopetoun had recommended John Adam (pl. 4), Robert's elder brother, and Robert himself, to the Earl of Dumfries, whose house (pl. 32) was already building as the travellers set forth.

The sculptor Joseph Wilton, who had studied and worked in Italy since 1747, introduced Adam to a 'most valuable and ingenious creature called Clérisseau who draws ruins in architecture to perfection' (pl. 17). It was a meeting of which Robert wrote, in a letter to his sister: 'I hope to reap some instruction from him . . . to study close with him and to purchase of his works'. Charles-Louis Clérisseau had lived at the French Academy in Rome for five years before he met Adam and had been a considerable friend to Adam's later rival, William Chambers. Robert quickly set up house in Rome and under Clérisseau's instruction and encouragement produced many of the Italian sketches of antique ruins (pls. 16, 18) and tumbled masonry (pl. 20). One of the most dramatic is from the 1756 group devoted to Hadrian's villa near Tivoli (pl. 19).

Sir John Summerson, Curator of Sir John Soane's Museum, where some 9,600 drawings by Robert and James Adam are preserved, has written percipiently of the Italian drawings:

> the freedom of these designs, the feeling that the artist is designing 'out of his head', the occasional introduction of Romanesque and Gothic themes, is very remarkable and something entirely new for English architecture. Adam was probably the first English architect consciously to break with the spirit of servitude to antiquity in this arrogant way. He knows he is, or is determined to be, a man of original genius.[1]

The many Soane 'Italian' drawings, and those in other collections, also show that almost everything that took the fancy was drawn – there was no dogmatic adherence to Roman forms. (The perceptive studies of Professor Alistair Rowan on the Adam castle style have drawn attention to many of these remembered Italian scenes reappearing in later years to influence the form of the Scottish castles.) While some scenes would perhaps have been drawn in the company of the mercurial Italian artist Giovanni Battista Piranesi – who dedicated a plate in his *Campus Martius* of 1762 to Adam 'with my head and his own joined' on it (pl. 10) – there was little of the Italian's style in them. The careful instructor was Clérisseau, with the execution of larger schemes of drawings such as those of the Roman baths of Diocletian and Caracalla helped along by Robert's draughtsmen Laurent-Benoit Dewez and Agostino Brunias. They were also working as a group almost full-time on the revision of Antoine Desgodetz's book *Les Édifices Antiques de Rome*, which had been available in many editions since its first publication in 1682.

Working at this hectic pace seems, fortuitously, to have prompted Robert Adam to abstract the essential details of antiquity and infuse them with a personal slant composed of many component pieces. The frequent excursions undertaken with Clérisseau and his draughtsmen into many parts of Italy for the work on the edition of Desgodetz produced a great number of drawings, most of them more accurate than those in the original volume. In fact the corrected measurements were to be printed in red ink, 'which lets them know the error', wrote Adam on 4 July 1755. But it was 'a work of years' as he told his brother James and his last six months in Rome were already to be busy enough, as he then knew. He had determined to go out from Venice to Dalmatia to visit the ruins – then unpublished – of Diocletian's palace at Spalato (*see* frontispiece).[2] Only shortage of money prevented this being the first point in an extended journey to Greece, and even Egypt and the Holy Land.

Within five weeks in July and August 1757, overriding lost permits and working constantly, the Palace was all measured. The main work fell on Clérisseau, although he was to be almost eclipsed in memory and recognition by Adam when the book finally appeared. Clérisseau was to supervise, with James Adam, the engraving of the plates in Venice, but difficulties with engravers, inaccuracies needing correction, the lack of money, and the appearance of the first volume of Stuart and Revett's book on Athens in 1762 delayed the whole volume. Robert Adam was already showing a business acumen, frustrating as he found the delay, by postponing his own volume's appearance until the fuss over Stuart and Revett's folio had died away. He also had to endure seeing the splendid presentation binding Stuart put on a few copies, two years ahead of his own, given to George III.[3]

At the centre of what Adam determined to do was a long and characteristic interest in 'movement' in architecture, which he had earlier discerned and approved of in the work of Sir John Vanbrugh, building at the start of the eighteenth century at Blenheim and elsewhere. In the first part of the *Works in Architecture* of 1773, where many of Robert Adam's opinions are set out, movement, it is explained, 'is meant to express the rise and fall, the advance and recess, with other diversity of form, in the different parts of a building, so as to add greatly to the picturesque of the composition'. In deciding what the 'Adam style' is we need to reckon then not only with lightness, smallness of ornament, colour, archaeological, Italian, French, and Renaissance influences, but with something more indefinable, with 'movement' in architecture. The wall or façade could be made to appear to fulfil the conditions of movement, and was frequently made to do so in the time of Baroque architects such as Borromini.

It allowed, in skilled hands, the creation of much that was novel, and Adam usually had before him the goal of complete originality, composed often out of banal elements. I say that he 'usually' had before him the goal of originality because we need to bear in mind a line or two from an interesting letter of 1756 written by Robert from Rome to his sister Margaret.[4] He asks for a set of best plans to be sent to him, and suggests Lord Braco's Duff House, which his father had begun in 1730; Yester, where both he and his father had worked; and Dumfries, which he had started before leaving on his tour. He wishes them sent so that by 'changing and shifting' he might receive inspiration for other things. The true eclectic was already at work.

We have noted Clérisseau's important work for Adam, although, as said, he was to be denied any credit in the great volume on Diocletian's palace when it was finally issued in 1764. He had instructed Adam both in French ways and in seeing at the sites in Dalmatia and Italy what was important as a reminder of a great and antique past. Adam knew that if he could sway patrons who had understood a little of what they had seen on their own Grand Tours with a reminder of a Roman style of interior decoration, and even of Etruscan art, he could achieve a new and acceptable mood. To all these component pieces he added a close study of Renaissance architecture, and of artists of the stature of Michelangelo. In particular, great villas, such as the wonderful unfinished creation of the Villa Madama of the 1520s, with its paintings, stuccoes, and grotesques, together with work by Raphael and his followers in the *Loggie* of the Vatican, encouraged him, as they did others, to study, copy, and recreate elements of them elsewhere. They were 200 years nearer in time to the Roman interiors than was his own age, and Adam realized that the Renaissance masters had had more chance to study a greater range of better-preserved antique remains in the sixteenth century than he could in the eighteenth.

All kinds of themes, without necessarily a continuity, but easy to interpret and accompanied by an inexhaustible variety of detail recalling the world of classical culture, became the light, poetic, and personal Adam style. There was no need to be modest and the Preface to the *Works* is filled with statements by the Adam brothers of what they could achieve through their studies. James made his own Italian tour from 1760 to 1762, accompanied by Clérisseau and the painter Antonio Zucchi. In fact the important words on 'movement' were first penned in an unpublished essay of November 1762 that James wrote on his return to London.

Robert and James stated in the *Works*:

We have introduced a great diversity of ceilings, freezes, and decorated pilasters, and have added grace and beauty to the whole by a mixture of grotesque, stucco and painted ornaments, together with the flowing rainceau, with its fanciful figures and winding foliage . . . we flatter ourselves we have been able to seize, with some degree of success, the beautiful spirit of antiquity, and to transfuse it, with novelty and variety, through all our numerous works.

While they erred in stating that they had 'not trod in the path of others, nor derived aid from their labours' they did make a completely personal style out of what they absorbed or adapted.

In the nearly four years he was in Italy, 1754–8, Robert Adam came to realize that the Romans had invested their buildings and interiors with a freedom of execution denied them by precise theorists and producers of books on antiquity in later years. This freedom, reticulation, expression of taste, and movement he carefully abstracted. Then he intensified and altered it as he thought expedient, and used it with flair, skill, and originality. He had been helped to see this freedom not only through his own observation and that of his friends and tutors but by the work of such artists and engravers as Santo Bartoli and Piranesi. There were also the ideas generated by the important series of books issued not only by Englishmen such as Robert Wood, but by the Frenchman le Comte de Caylus and his compatriot J. D. Le Roy. The Count published his magnificent illustrated work with the resounding title *Recueil d'Antiquités Egyptiennes, Étrusques, Grecques et Romaines* in 1752. He was followed by a whole series of volumes from Piranesi, including in 1757 the second issue of *Le Antiquità Romane* (first issued in 1748). Then in 1758 J. D. Le Roy published *Les Ruines des plus beaux monuments de la Grèce*. These volumes prefaced an extensive publication programme, and acrimonious debate, designed to assert the opposing claims for superiority of Roman or Greek architecture. This debate centred around the Abbé Wincklemann, who as a convert settled in Rome in 1755 and published his *Thoughts upon the Imitation of Greek Works of Art in Painting and Sculpture* in that year. The Abbé had a contempt for English 'milords', which seems to have kept him distant from Adam's circle (notwithstanding the nature of Wincklemann's ideas, which were unacceptable to many).

The Romans had built on a large scale and Adam had been able not only to see but to measure and have engraved the results of his observations. All he had to do when he returned to England was to apply the decorative repertory to 'many a small box of a house'. He knew that one of his principal tasks would be to compete against William Chambers, who had arrived back in England in 1755. That talented architect had a head-start in the form of Lord Bute's patronage, which had procured for him the post of architectural tutor to the Prince of Wales, afterwards George III. 'Bob the Roman' was presumably glad to be back to seek his own way and fortune.

II

A GREAT DIVERSITY OF WORK

On his return to London in January 1758 Adam was determined to make no sentimental journey north. He sent for James, and two of his sisters to keep house, to join him in London. After setting himself up in some style he was soon involved in the major task of devising decorations at Hatchlands, Surrey (pls. 33–5), for Admiral Edward Boscawen. It was the Admiral who also obtained for Adam the commission of the Admiralty Screen in Whitehall (pl. 42). It was inevitable that the Hatchlands work, coming at this early point, was a blend of Scottish and Italian memories. There were to be ruin paintings in panels all flanked by stucco arabesques. The design for the Drawing Room ceiling (pl. 34) also incorporated motifs to be found in the Villa Pamphili in Rome. It was a cautious and predictable start. He had yet to arrange into a cohesive whole the wide repertory of ornament – the profusion of rams' heads, urn shapes, griffins, paterae, anthemia, and other remembered elements of antique decoration.

Late in 1758, when engaged on the Hatchlands work, Robert wrote to James about the difficulty of finding 'English workmen who will leave their angly Stiff Sharp manner'. He had not as yet gathered around him those who could carry out his drawn ideas to perfection. But by the early 1760s the varied motifs were being incorporated into more assured versions of an elegant style – what in the *Works* the brothers were later to call 'a kind of revolution in the whole system of this useful and elegant art'. It soon commanded a growing patronage and with the help of the Duke of Argyll and Gilbert Elliot (later Lord Minto) Robert's name as a rising architect became better known. He could now engage William Chambers – who was not knighted until 1770 – on equal terms. In November 1761, within a year of George III's accession, they were both appointed Joint Architects of His Majesty's Works. This achievement brought to Adam an even more active private interest in his work. At Kedleston he was invited to supersede the other architects, Matthew Brettingham Jr and James Paine, who had worked at the north front of the house: the south (pl. 44) is an Adam creation in grand Roman style. Within a year or two of its commencement the owners of Bowood (pls. 50–5), Mersham Le Hatch (pls. 89–90), Croome (pls. 38–41), and Syon (pls. 79–87) were anxious for his attentions alone. He also began a grand town house, Lansdowne House, for Lord Shelburne in about 1761, although the Drawing Room (now re-erected in the Philadelphia Museum of Art – col. pl. 16) dates from six or seven years later. This work shows an early phase in the establishing of the Neo-Classical style, a style that matured in the mid 1760s and came into its most assured expression by the start of the 1770s.

It is hardly surprising that Adam's considerable achievement in influencing, for a time, the interior decoration of many English houses should tend to push his work on exteriors into shadow. Often, of course, he took over from other architects or worked at amending earlier houses; in addition, many of his exteriors have since been changed, demolished, or built over so completely to the designs of later architects that apart from those in castle style little of significance survives. Kedleston, the grandest Roman statement, is important; Mersham Le Hatch was built entirely to Adam's design by Thomas Cole; and there are a handful of houses that give a useful indication of what was possible. The great palace drawings (pl. 16) of the Italian years also give a hint of the great edifice he would have liked the King to emulate, however meanly, to his design. The Register House in Edinburgh (pls. 129–30) is a noble attempt at a great building, but although it was started towards the middle of the architect's career a mixture of committee indecision and parsimony prevented its realization in his lifetime.

The early houses often had porticos (pls. 36, 50) and a bold use of the Corinthian order. They lack the 'movement' he managed at Kedleston (pl. 44), where the facade was set out as part of the carefully contrived park scene (pl. 43), with attendant bridge, boat-houses, bath house, orange house, and entrance screen. As a final touch at Kedleston he gilded all the sash-bars of the windows on the outside of the house – it all attracted Dr Johnson's disapproval as consuming 'labour disproportionate to its utility', but this little concerned Adam's patrons. Perhaps the noblest exterior work, Kedleston apart, is to be seen in the amendments carried out at Osterley to the existing house. The great portico (pls. 56–8) binds the façade together and the house earned rapturous praise as the 'palace of palaces' from Horace Walpole.

In the decade 1770–80 the interiors grew richer while the exteriors, particularly of the town houses, became plainer, were covered in stucco, or set out like the Adelphi (pl. 114) in monotonous repetition. There were occasional controlled successes, like 20 Portman Square (pl. 133), which displays an interesting use of brick and Coade-stone decoration. The façades of the small town-planning schemes in Charlotte Square, Edinburgh (pl. 155), and the late work in London at Fitzroy Square (pl. 154), also show a concern for symmetry and balance that has often been abandoned by later users and emenders of Adam's work. Indeed, Adam may perhaps be appraised as an architect with a surpassing eye for symmetry, nowhere better displayed than at Gunton church, Norfolk – in the small classical façade (pl. 117) – or at the Mausoleum, Bowood (pl. 55). On many occasions of course Adam had to work with an existing structure, where room for innovation was, to a greater or lesser extent, limited; at other times, as in the great schemes for altering the layout of King's College, Cambridge, the work came to almost nothing.

In his early years of practice recommendations were vital to Adam. It was on the basis of favourable remarks such as the one made in a letter of 1758 by Lady Mary Wortley Montagu to her friend the Countess of Bute[5] that the commissions began to appear; but it was still to take another five hard years to consolidate the business. A bank account was opened with Drummonds in 1764. It had a balance of £6,620 in that year, but by 1768 this had increased to £12,359, and by 1771 it was at a little over £40,000. We shall note, however, how success was nearly turned into bankruptcy by the ill-fated Adelphi scheme (pl. 114).

One of the patrons most ready to recognize the skill and talent of Robert Adam was the 6th Earl of Coventry, who was building at Croome Court, Worcestershire. The Adam accounts for the work, neatly tabulated on folio sheets, begin in August 1760 with 'an elevation and plan of the Greenhouse or Orangery (£5 15s)', and the first 'Design of a Ceiling for the Gallery' was sub-mitted in September at £12 12s. This was speedily rejected – the large box of working drawings at Kedleston, all of which were charged for, shows how money could be extracted quickly from a client who frequently changed his mind – and in March 1761 'A new design [as executed] for the ceiling of the Gallery' finds its place at £9 9s. It was intended to fit up the Gallery as a Library (pl. 40). In May 1761 an 'Elevation and Plan of a Bridge (£5 15s.)' preceded the 'Sections of the Inside Finishings of the Gothic Church'. The 'new' church at Croome, in which material from the old church appears to have been incorporated, was designed by the landscape gardener and architect Lancelot 'Capability' Brown, but we know that his work was 'confined to the carcase' while the internal treat-ment (pl. 91), as in the case of the principal rooms of the house, was handed over to Adam.

Adam visited Croome regularly and a month after his October 1763 visit drawn sections of the Tapestry Room (col. pl. 2), a room now re-erected at the Metropolitan Museum, New York, were sent for Lord Coventry's approval. Coventry had visited the Gobelins tapestry manufactory in France in August 1763 and had ordered a set of Boucher-Neilson tapestries. Adam provided a design for their disposition at Croome. Coventry was one of a small group of patrons who patronized the Gobelins manufactory – William Weddell at Newby also ordered a set from them (col. pl. 30) and later Robert Child did so for Osterley (col. pl. 6). Lord Coventry's tapestries were not woven and ready until 1771, by which time the Tapestry Room ceiling on fir laths was painted bluish-white, and the chimneypiece had been given a red Veronese-marble background and trims in white and lapis-lazuli.

Schemes such as this certainly overturned the prevailing monotony of most English interior decoration. French interest in developments in England – sharpened after isolation in the Seven Years' War – and the extensive transfer of Adam's influence on design to that country, was in a minor way reversed when in 1767 Adam designed a Tripod 'altered from a French Design for a water stand'. But while he had probably talked to Francophiles such as Lord Coventry and Sir Henry Bridgeman about introducing classical tripods into decorative schemes prior to this date, he had, in fact, been anticipated by James Stuart's splendid ormolu example of about 1760 at Kedleston. Stuart's example was noted in the mid 1760s by that indefatigable traveller and recorder the Duchess of Northumberland, for whom Adam was working, through her husband the 1st Duke, at Syon House.

Syon was a most important commission: Summerson has suggested that 'the gallery at Syon [1764] may . . . be the place where the Adam style was actually initiated' (col. pls. 12–14; pl. 85). This room, in its nervous run-away length, has the basic structure of a narrow Jacobean long gallery. It presented Adam with special problems because of its meagre width, a disability he overcame by a brilliant use of Corinthian pilasters, sixty-two of them, which draw the eye to the space they flank: as the architect said, the gallery 'was finished in a style to afford great variety and amusement'. It was a carefully contrived system of verticals and horizontals – the ceiling lozenges are left incomplete as they join the wall, almost as if one could pop one's head through a door to see them emerge at the other side. It was another device to give an illusion of width, and was part of the careful and individual attention that Adam added to his assured knowledge of interior decoration. Contrasted with the great heavy majestic Hall (pl. 83) at Syon of 1761 the change is remarkable. It shows that despite breaking away gradually over the next few years from heaviness to assured lightness of touch he was already capable of doing so when the occasion demanded. The Syon Gallery stands as testimony to this achievement.

Adam's patron, the 1st Duke of Northumberland (pl. 85), was typical of that breed of intelligent noblemen to whose capabilities artists such as Chippendale could refer. When dedicating his pattern-book *The Director* to the Duke Chippendale wrote of His Grace's 'intimate acquaintance with all the arts and sciences that tend to perfect and adorn life'. The Duke's interests ranged from Egyptian sculpture to Italian Renaissance painting; he knew unerringly when an architectural order was wrongly applied, and as he told Robert Adam in November 1764: 'I must desire you will order those Carved Mouldings which have been so ill executed by Mr Adair to be returned him & amended in such a manner as you shall approve of for I would not, upon any account suffer any work to be fixed up at Sion that is not completely finished to your satisfaction'. The efforts of the craftsmen in translating such ducal edicts into effective patterns, and to acceptable standards, is examined later in section III. That most of them succeeded in the intricate detailing of Syon is undeniable.

By the late 1760s the commissions were plentiful and work sometimes continued for as long as twenty years on the same house – Adam was still supplying drawings for work at Croome in 1781. The aim was to suit each patron's individual taste as far as possible by the putting together and taking away of a number of common parts for each scheme. The arrangement of the wall and ceiling surface at various commissions shows this at work. In respect of the walls, the hall at Osterley (pl. 59), that at Syon (pl. 83), and the Gallery at Croome (pl. 40) all include pilasters or enriched columns, niches or apses containing sculpture, and classical panels, and yet are of a basically flat treatment. The heaviness of these early designs with their florid decoration, variety of friezes and decorative panels, and columns with rich entablatures (pl. 84) was in a grand Roman manner.

Robert Adam's Italian drawings often show the kind of panels that are a common feature in the interiors. The long plaques of decorative flowing ornament in the Ante-Room at Syon (col. pl. 15) and the Gallery at Croome (pl. 40), the ruin scenes that were provided at many houses from the 1760s (col. pls. 20, 23), and the grotesque panels (pl. 61) in the Entrance Hall at Osterley are typical of many variations on the theme of bringing together all the disparate elements. The great full-length trophy panels at Syon (col. pl. 15) and Osterley and effective room schemes like the entrance hall at Newby (col. pl. 31) – where the plasterwork is dated 1771 on a small section of a panel – are by contrast not common. The use of small plaques and medallions can be seen in the library at Kenwood (col. pl. 34) and the Long Gallery at Harewood; these were easier to place around walls and to set in plaster, or as oil-on-canvas or paper roundels into ceilings (col. pls. 18, 28). All around were plaster reliefs of urns, singly or in groups, swags, griffins, and sphinxes, which enlivened in a precise array.

The most unusual of the wall treatments was that which was a part of the 'Etruscan' rooms. In the *Works* Adam stated, after a paragraph or two on Etruscan vases and their colouring, that 'long before their acquaintance with the Greeks, the Romans had derived from Etruria such information as enabled them to make a very considerable progress in many branches of architecture'. He went on to say that it was nevertheless remarkable that neither in Hadrian's villa, where so much attention was paid to elegance and variety, nor in any part of Herculaneum or Pompeii 'has any fragment been yet produced of interior decoration, executed in the taste now before us'. He produced some eight rooms in the 'Etruscan' style of which the dressing room at Osterley (col. pl. 8; pls. 69–74) is the only substantial survival. It shows the stage Adam had reached by the mid 1770s of unifying a design, of relating the doors (pls. 70–1) to the detail of the walls and even to the chimneyboard (pl. 74). The carpet no longer survives, but echoed the same spirit of decoration with the same colourful variety of detail that is found on the ceiling (col. pl. 8). We have noted Adam's interest in the pattern and colouring of Etruscan vases but the main inspiration for the Etruscan room decoration seems to have come from Piranesi's *Diverse Maniere D'Adornare I Cammini* of 1769 (pl. 72).

The arrangement of this colourful room at Osterley, with its sensitive arabesques, allows a few words on colour in Adam interiors. In the *Works* the Adams say:

> We have thought it proper to colour with the tints, used in the execution a few copies of each number, not only that posterity might be enabled to judge with more accuracy concerning the taste of the present age, and that foreign connoisseurs might have it in their power to indulge their curiosity with respect to our national style of ornament; but that the public in general might have an opportunity of cultivating the beautiful art of decoration, hitherto so little understood in most of the countries of Europe.

The researches of Ian Bristow on ready-mixed paint in the eighteenth century list the problems:[6] grinding pigment into the oil was slow and laborious, even more so when done *in situ*; machines, horse-mills to grind the colours, speeded it up but led to the point where Robert Campbell in 1747 in *The London Tradesmen* complained that the trade of painting 'is now at a very low ebb'. Adam was anxious to colour with the various tints 'to take off the crudeness of the white', which hitherto had been the obligatory colour for all plaster and stucco decoration, with the occasional judicious addition of gilded ornaments.

The richness of the Adam colour repertory is effectively demonstrated by the drawings made prior to execution of the work: thirteen examples of these are reproduced as colour plates in this book. They date for the most part from after 1765 and include a fine example, published here for the first time, of the Drawing Room ceiling at Newby (col. pl. 32) of about 1771.

The usual place for colour in early Adam interiors was on the ceiling but it was introduced at first in a subdued way. By the late 1760s, as at Kenwood (col. pl. 34), for example, the walls were more colourful and demanded stronger ceiling patterning and a close integration of all the elements, such as in the work at Saltram (col. pl. 35).

The complexities of an Adam colour scheme are best followed by a serious student in the drawings at Sir John Soane's Museum, and in such meticulously detailed records as that compiled about the installation and re-colouring of the ceiling from Garrick's house in the Adelphi at the Victoria & Albert Museum. What emerged in this exercise, among much else of great value, was the faithfulness of the colours in the drawing (col. pl. 37) to the decoration of the room itself, a surprising enough finding bearing in mind the usual fading of colours over the years. Pale pastel tints there may be in profusion in Adam's drawings but can one deny the strength and clarity of the colours in the design for the carpet at Mrs Montagu's house in Hill Street, *c.* 1766 (col. pl. 26)? The strong blue in the drawing dominates, but equally bright and effective colours may be found even in the smaller objects such as the drawing for a firescreen for Mrs Child of Osterley (col. pl. 7).

Apart from the richness of colour in the drawings, the translation of them to the actual rooms can be seen to have been effectively accomplished: at Harewood, for example, the archives show that the house-painter Thomas Sunderland was busy painting to the guidance of prepared drawings in September 1769. Several of his men were painting in the Hall and the Music Room '& laying on specimen of Colours for Mr Adam's approbation'. This approval was also necessary for the decoration of the well-known Ante-Room at Syon (col. pl. 15), with its gilded stucco decorations, blue, green, red, and cream pavement, and the blue and gold trophy panels. But this is an early room – about 1762 – and the ceiling, while a rich display, relies on the use of gilded foliation set against a white ground. We have noted that this restraint was soon altered, and in many settings colour took over the whole of the wall and ceiling decorations.

The work in composition plaster was usually done by Joseph Rose & Company (pp. 20–1) at the Adam commissions. What did they do in helping to arrange the decoration of ceilings? While the construction of any room usually consists of a ceiling, three or more walls, and a floor, it was the ceiling in Adam interiors that had the unifying effect. This was because the carpet design often copied the ceiling, and at Saltram (col. pl. 35) and Harewood (col. pl. 20) this feature is particularly effective. The early forms were what Adam in the *Works* called a 'Compartment ceiling' – 'a name given to all ceilings that are divided into various pannels, surrounded with mouldings'. After some strictures on all the ancient coffered forms, some of which he had seen at first hand in Rome, he goes on to say that 'it seems to have been reserved for the present times to see compartment ceilings, and those of every kind, carried to a degree of perfection in Great Britain, that far surpasses any of the former attempts of other modern nations'. While Adam's work at Croome and Bowood may have paid some attention to this form he was largely critical of compartmental ceilings and goes on, in his now oft-quoted phrase, to talk of having introduced in its place 'a great diversity of ceilings, freezes and decorated pilasters'. There are of course occasional stylistic oddities. The Eating Room ceiling at Osterley and the Dining Room one at Shardeloes have oval ribs across which wreathing vine leaves twist. At Osterley there are no Adam designs for the Eating Room, and it has been thought possible the work could have been carried out for William Chambers in the pre-Adam phase of Osterley's building. However, the work should I think remain with Adam – there is a similar ceiling at Apsley House, Piccadilly, which is undeniably by the Scottish architect. What is much more typical of Adam are those ceilings in which paintings in lozenge and roundel form are incorporated: there are mature examples at Harewood (col. pl. 18), 20 St James's Square, London (col. pl. 44), and Nostell (col. pl. 22).

The ceilings in Adam schemes of decoration have been placed in five main categories:[7]

(a) simple concentric oval and circular rings, of which the Entrance Hall ceiling at Osterley (pl. 60) is an example of the basic form
(b) an arrangement and division of the concentric rings or ovals by enrichments in plaster or composition (pl. 90)
(c) ceilings in which a central motif in plaster (pl. 122) or paint (col. pl. 28) is emphasized
(d) tripartite patterns in which two end sections flank a larger central square or rectangle (col. pl. 32)
(e) overall patterns, of which many versions abound (col. pls. 38, 48).

A sixth version may be allowed where enrichment of a cove (col. pl. 11) or apse (pl. 80) is involved. A very flamboyant and unique example of decoration of a cove is that in the Drawing Room at Syon (col. pl. 11), with its inserted painted roundels by Giovanni Battista Cipriani. The variety of Adam ceilings can be traced in the many surviving drawings. Even the provincial plasterer found himself able to imitate much that was in the Adam style when George Richardson (c. 1736–1813) issued his A Book of Ornamental Ceilings in the style of the Antique Grotesque in 1776; in the preface Richardson, who had accompanied James Adam on his Grand Tour, 1760–3, stated that he had been for eighteen years draughtsman and designer to those eminent masters Messrs Adam of the Adelphi.

It was the Adelphi building project that almost brought ruin to the brothers. The scheme had long been in mind of raising a great 'palace' upon the mudbanks of waste land in the Durham Yard area of Westminster, near the Thames. To set houses with fine river views above a wharf with large warehouses beneath the terrace seemed a splendid idea, but their friend David Hume thought otherwise: 'the scheme of the Adelphi always appeared so imprudent that my wonder is how they could have gone on so long'. In 1769 the brothers petitioned for Parliamentary sanction – Robert had been the Member for Kinross-shire since 1768 – and their efforts were supported not only by their friends and most of their fellow Scots but also by the King and Lord North. They were opposed by the livery companies of watermen and lightermen and by the City of London. Adam spoke once, on 20 March 1771, to counter the charge that the Bill was being rushed along by 'parliamentary craft'.

Professor Alistair Rowan has traced the financial rigours that surrounded the Adelphi in a carefully researched paper,[8] but for a time none were too apparent to the Adam brothers. They soon found, however, that the houses did not sell, despite their friend Garrick taking No. 6 (col. pl. 37), Adam living in No. 4 (col. pl. 36; pl. 116), and Josiah Wedgwood wanting a pottery showroom there. From about 1778 all that the brothers earned from their practice as architects was swallowed up by their company's debts. Horace Walpole, who had earlier praised 'the taste and skill of Mr Adam . . . famed for public works' wished that 'the constellation of the Adelphi' should be 'rayée from the celestial globe'. The scheme depended on the Government leasing the underbuildings, but because of rumours of flooding this did not come about. Their nephew William described it as a time when 'the underground stream of loss and expenditure . . . gradually sapped and finally overset them'.

The brothers had tried to raise funds by a loan on the family estate and the Christie's sale of their art collection but these efforts produced insufficient money. In May 1773 they petitioned Parliament again for permission to dispose of all their assets (except the estate) by a lottery – a popular enough eighteenth-century pastime. After a long debate a Bill allowing this, and sponsored again by friends, including William Pulteney of Bath, passed both Houses. The lottery itself was a success and prizes even came to the brothers, who held unsold tickets. It freed them from their immediate debts, and with a considerable portion of their art collection bought in (to appear in the 1818 and 1821 sales) they could look forward, tainted, but with cautious optimism. They were saved from complete bankruptcy by the large scale of their business. The Adelphi was demolished in 1936: its arches (pl. 115) and fragments remain (col. pl. 36).

The Adelphi was the only piece of sustained town planning completed to the brothers' designs in their lifetimes. Later alterations to the Portland Place scheme, and those of 1790 in Fitzroy Square (pl. 154), focus attention north to one of their few complete schemes, to the development of Charlotte Square (pl. 155), in their native capital of Edinburgh. In the scheme there is a reference back to the Adelphi façade (pl. 114) with its pediment and ordered regularity. Robert likewise introduced regularity and a central pediment into Pulteney Bridge at Bath (pl. 118), the only part of William Pulteney's Bathwick estate to be built. But in Edinburgh there was also a chance to be innovative, and some grand drawings (pls. 149–50) resulted. The buildings, the General Register House (pl. 130), for example, have often been much altered by later architects and builders.

The Adam brothers maintained a separate Scottish office, and Robert made annual trips north, of a month or so, each summer. On one of these, very late in his life, the University building (pl. 151) was started. It is now much added to and was different even then from the time of '45 when Adam had been a student there. Charlotte Square was not finished until Adam had been long dead, the great church being erected by Sir Robert Reid from 1811 to 1814, with flanking houses to Adam's original design.

Two further aspects of the great diversity of work we have been describing need to be considered. One, the moveable furniture, silver, carpets, and other examples of craftsmanship, is related to the work of its creators in section III. The other is the important Scottish castles, with their allusion to the early interests Adam had in the Gothic and the picturesque.

The castle style was unique and has been studied by a few writers, and notably by Professor Alistair Rowan.[9] The early Adam studies in this genre remained, like many of the remembered wonders of Italian palaces, as impressive drawings only (pl. 16). The first castle of significance, and probably of actuality, was that built from 1764 at Ugbrooke in Devon for the 4th Lord Clifford (pl. 92). It is a large castellated box with an attractive bow and towers at each corner. The windows show that element of 'movement' referred to earlier (p. 5), an effect caused by setting the ground-floor windows within relieving arches, with the central bays advancing into the shallow two-storey bow. The square style was followed at Mellerstain in the 1770s (pl. 120), where William Adam had worked on the central block in 1725, a date carved on the base of the east wing. A more remarkable castle for 'movement' was, however, that built about 1770 for Patrick Home at Wedderburn, near Duns. Wedderburn Castle (pl. 123) has a rusticated ground storey, octagonal towers at each corner, which rise about the general roof-line, and a central bowed projection. The play of sun and shade across this imposing facade does much to create an effect of 'movement'. The effect of each castle design usually seems enhanced by the combination of its massing and the variety of its forms, something that is particularly true of the south front of Culzean Castle (col. pl. 49), built from 1777 on the Ayrshire coast for the 10th Earl of Cassillis. The attractive interior includes one of the most imposing staircases (col. pl. 51) in any eighteenth-century house, rivalling in its daring and well-constructed oval form that by William Kent in London at 44 Berkeley Square.

At Oxenfoord Castle there is later work by William Burn to contend with – although Burn was a talented architect. The garden façade (pl. 147) is nearest to Adam and with its large bow it draws attention to that same feature at Dalquharran Castle, Ayrshire (pl. 148), of 1785, recently made a ruin, and at Pitfour, Perthshire (pl. 152), built about 1790 for John Richardson. Both have boldly accented towers and prominent bays, but with a central stair and cupola, a square hall and saloon, are really arranged to a traditional villa plan.

The last of the Castle Houses to which we must refer is Seton, built in East Lothian for an Edinburgh lawyer between 1789 and 1791. Sir John Summerson has written that 'the house builds up like an operatic set beyond the low gateway and outworks. The fact that it is really quite a small house with a specially generous front door makes its castellar pretensions the more transparent and appealing'.[10] It is as seemingly fortified as Vanbrugh's Seaton Delaval. As Adam thought a great deal of Vanbrugh, and called his buildings 'rough jewels of inestimable value', the debt at Seton to the bold massing effects achieved by the Baroque architect is clear. But as an eclectic to the end Adam also remembered the great Papal fortifications in Italy, and his own windswept fortifications at Fort George.

There are over forty castle designs. In all of them are hybrid elements gathered from many sources – the small garden tower at Auchincruive (pl. 146) is based on Theodoric's mausoleum at Ravenna – and in all of them he played about with recession, with battlements, with conical roofs, ball finials, towers, and arches, to make as original a contribution to architecture as he had to decoration. After his death the editor of the *Gentleman's Magazine*, Cave, a personal friend, wrote in the obituary notice (July 1792): 'The loss of Mr Adam at this time must be peculiarly felt, as the new University of Edinburgh, and other great public works, both in that city and in Glasgow were erecting from his designs, and under his direction'.

Contemporaries seem to have judged Robert Adam as a sensible person, a lively conversationalist, liberal-minded, but not a little vain. He kept the patronage and friendship of many of the leading men of his day. That he lost the favour of George III – a fact that the King commented on in a letter to Lord North in June 1777 – was almost entirely due to the intrigues of Sir William Chambers.

The funeral procession was attended by distinguished pall-bearers: the Duke of Buccleuch, the Earl of Coventry, the Earl of Lauderdale, the Viscount Stormont, Lord Frederick Campbell, and William Pulteney; his coffin was laid beneath a plain slab in the south transept of Westminster Abbey. Near to it, equally undistinguished, are the tombs of Sir William Chambers and James Wyatt, his rivals, imitators, and on occasion superiors, who helped in their own way to render the Neo-Classical style something so effective that it carried on to younger generations, and in a debased form to the present day.

It was of course inevitable that in the last years there were many imitators of the Adam style, and also many waspish detractors. Chambers, Wyatt, Robert Smirke senior, C. H. Tatham, and Joseph Gwilt were among those who had cheap jibes to throw out – 'white walls with which Mr Adam has speckled this city. They are no better than Models for a Twelfth-Night Decoration of a Pastry Cook' is a typical example, and it all went on long after Robert's death.

Despite the detractors the Adam style spread to Russia, Ireland, and America. The penetration of the style into Russia was entirely owed to a fellow Scotsman, Charles Cameron (*c.* 1740–1812), who, styling himself as 'Architect', had also visited Italy. In 1770 he issued proposals for 'publishing by subscription in one volume folio' a book on the Roman thermae. He stated that he had studied under the correct Palladian Isaac Ware, and, like Robert Adam with the Diocletian folio, he hoped that the 'credit arising to him from it will compensate for the labour and expence he has been at in the prosecution of such an arduous undertaking'.

About 1778 Cameron was invited to Russia, where he worked for Catherine the Great at Tsarskoe Selo, using Scottish craftsmen who had been advertised for in Edinburgh. The rest of his life was spent in Russia. Whilst in casual terms he may be thought an Adam imitator – his Grecian Hall at Pavlovsk (1780) was inspired by Adam's work at Kedleston – he brought to his drawing a competent architectural training and sure technique based on first-hand observation; indeed it could be said that he did more than Adam in this respect, who had relied at Spalato on the researches and drawings by Clérisseau.

In 1770 Lord Bective had asked Adam to rebuild his house at Headfort in Ireland. The architect did little in Ireland, but Headfort was erected despite many alterations to the drawings, which are dated between 1771 and 1775. The eating parlour was to have Clérisseau-type ruins in panels, but this scheme was not carried out and the design for finishing the four sides of the hall was clearly done by a less capable hand. At Powerscourt House, Dublin, the stuccoists James McCullagh, Michael Reynolds, and Michael Stapleton enriched the walls with Adamesque-style work. This had been spread abroad by the pattern-books, McCullagh's own, George Richardson's book of 1776 on the Antique Grotesque ceilings, and various titles issued by the Milanese architect Placido Columbani, who was resident in England. They were popular purchases with stuccoists and carvers, and the work at Lucan House and the staircase and Organ Room of 1785 by Stapleton at Belvedere College, Dublin, are good examples of how effective the transference could be.

The movement, like many Irish stuccoists, moved westwards to America. Charles Bulfinch (1763–1844), a gentleman of education and standing, had been able to study the Adam style on his Grand Tour when he visited England, France, and Italy. His architectural career was thus influenced by what he had seen, and in an America that was soon to turn to the emulation of Greek buildings he built and decorated several houses in the 'Adam way'. The Senate Chamber of the Massachusetts State House of 1795, for which Bulfinch was responsible, has very fine late-eighteenth-century plasterwork. The plasterer Daniel Raynard, who did much of this work in New England, also collaborated in 1806 with Asher Benjamin to produce *The American Builder's Companion*, which cribbed liberally from English sources. This book was of the utmost use, along with the popular circulation of many other English pattern books, to builders such as Bulfinch and Samuel McIntire (1757–1811) in spreading the Adam style in eastern America. The *Works in Architecture* volumes of 1773 and 1779, which had done so much for the Adam brothers' own reputations, were also very influential after the Revolution. Even Thomas Jefferson, who had in his own architectural work an almost unswerving allegiance to Palladio, included on his shelves a copy of Desgodetz's book on the antiquities of Rome. When he acquired it, in 1791, many humbler works in a similar vein, particularly the books for builders and joiners issued by William Pain, would already have been available. Composition ornaments for mantelpieces and doorcases were sent out from England, moulded in Adam style. Mrs Coade's London manufactory was also sending medallions and chimneypieces in the popular artificial 'Coade stone'. These decorative elements were put together in rooms in the form of convincing be-swagged chimneypieces and pilasters and panels, which often incorporated mythological figures modelled after Flaxman's originals for Wedgwood.

The Adam influence in America[11] began properly in the 1780s, was dominant in the 1790s and early nineteenth century, and was then freely modified by the publication of Benjamin's book in 1806. But by the mid 1820s Greek forms reigned triumphant and they gradually replaced all that was Adamitic and that spoke only of Rome.

III

'A REGIMENT OF ARTIFICERS'[12]

The part played by the craftsmen in the creation of the Adam style is gradually emerging from a period of being overshadowed by the splendours of the work itself. The principal years of Adam's activity coincided with the important new influence on artistic training that came with the foundation of the Royal Academy Schools in 1768. Hitherto training in England for the crafts consisted of apprenticeship, with examinations carried out by the Livery Companies to determine proficiency. There was no organization that set a standard in design, or encouraged individual lines of experiment or development. In the early eighteenth century Sir Godfrey Kneller and Sir James Thornhill supported the St Martin's Lane Academy, which was continued by Thornhill's son-in-law, William Hogarth. This academy had influential members, some of whom seem to have made an important contribution to the advancement of the Rococo style, but the Hogarth-directed academy did not have much effect on the training of students, and a deteriorating situation over the next twenty years brought, finally, the presentation of a petition to George III requesting him to set up a new Academy School; it was signed by twenty-two artists and architects. Adam was not one of the signatories but his rival William Chambers was, and the list also included the signatures of many of the decorative painters whom Adam patronized, such as Cipriani, Angelica Kauffmann, and Francesco Zuccarelli. The patronage that resulted from the presentation of the petition founded the Royal Academy and laid down the basis for its Schools. Of the 1,551 pupils admitted in the period 1768–1830 almost half (771) were painters, and the remainder consisted of architects (247), designers (3), draughtsmen (4), engravers, and sculptors. Perhaps one of the most significant names, for our purpose, to appear in these lists was that of Joseph Rose junior (1745–99), who was to take his place in the family firm of plasterers as one of Robert Adam's most dependable craftsmen (pl. 108). In 1768 he visited Italy with influential companions, including the landscape painters James Forrester and George Robertson, Mr and Mrs Richard Dalton, Gavin Hamilton, Peter de Angelis, and Joseph Nollekens the sculptor, who was later to have the morbid duty of taking Adam's death mask. Dalton had been sent to Italy by George III to collect pictures for the royal collections. Returning to England, Rose entered the Royal Academy Schools in 1770 and was admitted a member of the Worshipful Company of Plasterers in 1775. The Rose family firm had already served Robert Adam from as early as 1760 and Joseph junior was probably present at most of the early Adam commissions, such as Croome, despite being still in his teens.

The growing success and spread of the Adam style brought much acclaim and success to the architect, but did it come to his craftsmen? In the case of the Rose family and the important cabinet-makers, sculptors, and decorative painters there seems little doubt that their incomes were considerable. Joseph Rose senior was in a position, when he died in 1780, to leave £6,000 to each of his nephews, and the cabinet-maker John Cobb and the sculptor Henry Cheere, successful craftsmen, had healthy bank accounts at Drummonds, where Adam's own account was kept. It may well be that the provision of classic order and discipline paid a craftsman well, even if fertility of invention had to be sacrificed to the rule and precedent of Neo-Classicism.

One of the important factors in Adam's success was the overall control he gave to the integration of movable objects in their setting. The plates in the *Works* in particular (pl. 157) show the attention given to small items of door furniture, window catches, cornices, and so on. He was seeking to establish a synthesis in which everything, furniture, carpets, and fittings, bore the impress of a single directing mind within the compass of an all-embracing style. The only way he was able to do this was by setting up an efficient office organization and employing skilled draughtsmen such as George Richardson.

The work of the offices in London and Scotland was organized by the setting up of William Adam & Company in 1764. It remained in being until 1801. The company was responsible for building both the Adelphi (*Adelphoi* is Greek for brothers) and the Royal Society of Arts (pl. 112). The architectural practice Robert and James had set up largely occupied their attention, leaving the younger William to manage the Company. The elder brother, John, stayed in Scotland, busy with his own affairs, having granted a power of attorney to James, who seems to have been responsible for contacts with a wide range of patrons and committees.

For an eighteenth-century business William Adam & Company operated on a lavish scale. The biographical notice of Robert that appeared in the *Scots Magazine* of May 1803 said that they had over 2,000 men working for them, while David Hume in a letter of 27 June 1772 to Adam Smith set the figure at 3,000 or more and said 'they must dismiss them'. They had a timber business and stock of wood, brickworks in London and Essex, shares in a firm of builders' suppliers, a stone and paving business, and John had interests in Aberdeen granite quarries that sent their stone to London to pave the streets. Had all of these enterprises been well managed the run on them at the time of the Adelphi crisis might well have been avoided and the problems of their patent stucco monopoly minimized. I have discussed this problem elsewhere;[13] briefly, the friend for whom they had built at Kenwood, the 1st Earl of Mansfield, gave a sympathetic hearing to their case of 1778 about a rival stucco composition, and found for them. However, they had frequent actions over the failure of their Liardet composition used for facing houses. The sand business, part of William Adam & Company, also ended in failure. Soon the architectural gains were all being lost.

From about 1772 the brothers mantained a separate Edinburgh drawing office as well as the London one. They had a clerk of works in charge – at first James Salisbury and then, after 1788, John Paterson. They had some three men who visited and surveyed sites, copied designs sent up from the Adelphi office, kept an eye on the increasing number of Scottish commissions, and acted for the brothers at meetings over the development of the 'New Town' in Edinburgh.

The vast number of surviving Adam drawings is an indication that there was a large team of draughtsmen in the London office. However, there is equally little doubt of Robert's own abundant energy, as the main rough outline sketches surviving in the collection at Sir John Soane's Museum testify. The usual practice seemed to be to make two sets of drawings, often following Adam's charcoal sketch on which notations for all the colours were entered. The first set, usually on Whatman paper, would go to the client, the second was filed, and used as the one to be 'pricked through' to form an outline for further copies. Many of the drawings bear figured dimensions and inscriptions recording their purpose and for whom intended: 'Organ Case for Sir Nathanial Curzon, Bart', for example. Others bear notes, such as that of 1767 concerning a carpet for Lord Coventry's octagonal dressing-room at his London house, 29 Piccadilly: 'Mr Adam has not had time to fix the colours of the border, but thinks that need not stop the estimate from being made. When that is fixt, if the drawing is returned to Mr Adam he will settle the other parts of the colouring'. Several drawings were, however, completely coloured to a high standard, and were of a complexity and richness that allowed no competitors or copyists.

Lord Coventry, in 1764, queried the cost of some of these drawings, but, as an unpublished letter of 3 April shows, Adam was adept at countering such complaints:

> I am extrimely sorry your Lordship should have thought of deducting any part of the Money, as almost every person I have done designs for, upon considering that it is my only branch of Business, and that I have never stated a sixpence for Surveying . . . have generally sent me, a present over and above the Bill itself.

He went on to indicate what sums he had received over the amount of his bill, how he had spent out on acquiring his knowledge, and hoped Lord Coventry would not deduct anything from the submitted account. The case was argued firmly and politely and Lord Coventry paid the same day!

Robert Adam's bank account at Drummonds Bank gives the names of several of the craftsmen he employed. On their abilities much of his reputation rested, and the following list, by the consistent reappearance of their names in the account, and in house archives, probably represents competent craftsmen in frequent employment:[14]

Bricklayer	Edward Gray
Mason/Sculptor	John Devall
Plasterers	Joseph Rose & Company
Carvers and Joiners	John Adair, Oliver and Sefferin Alken, Richard Collins, John Gilbert, John Hobcraft, John Phillips, Saffron Nelson

Metal and Coppersmiths	William Kinsman, Thomas Tilston
Locksmith	Thomas Blockley
Plumbers	George Shakespear, William Chapman.

Together with this efficient group there were the associations with a talented body of cabinet-makers, silversmiths, carpet weavers, upholsterers, and other craftsmen of various specialized trades. The decorative painters formed a significant group of itinerant foreigners and their activities are discussed below. They were all ready to follow out the colour drawings 'at large' from the London office and their joint attendance at the early stages of a commission has been well summarized in the comment of Mrs Montagu in a letter of 20 July 1779 to her friend the Duchess of Portland:

> Mr Adam came at the head of a regiment of artificers an hour after the time he had promised; the bricklayer talked about the alterations to be made in a wall; the stonemason was as eloquent about the coping of the said wall; the carpenter thought the internal fitting-up of the house not less important; then came the painter, who is painting my ceilings in various colours, according to the present fashion.

No Adam interior after the early years was complete without painted decoration, and it is necessary to discuss briefly the more important artists. They did on occasion work for architects such as Chambers or Wyatt, but to the casual mind their colourful achievements are mainly related to Robert Adam's designs.

In addition to the foreigners there were also some native decorators whom Adam patronized, but it is with such foreign painters as Angelica Kauffmann, her third husband Antonio Zucchi, Giovanni Battista Cipriani, Michele Angelo Pergolesi, and Biagio Rebecca that we should concern ourselves. Many decorations in Adam interiors have been carelessly attributed to Angelica Kauffmann (1741–1807), probably because documented ceiling paintings by her are very rare. Born in Switzerland, she trained in Italy, and came to England in the early years of Adam's important building activities. As a foundation member of the Royal Academy – there are authenticated ceiling paintings by her at Burlington House – she showed regularly at the annual exhibitions. Her engravings were also used as the basis of decorative work on furniture, and for Matthew Boulton's 'mechanical paintings process'.[15] She finally left England for Italy in 1781, the year in which she married.

Antonio Zucchi (1726–95), Angelica's husband, was probably employed by Robert Adam in 1757 to engrave plates for the *Spalatro* book, and at the architect's invitation he later came to England. He appears many times as a payee in Robert Adam's bank account, on one occasion, in 1770, for £1,000. In England Zucchi centred himself on London and was much visited by prospective patrons. Therese Parker, *née* Robinson, writing to her brother Frederick in London on 17 September 1769, asks that he call about the pictures commissioned from Zucchi by her husband, John Parker, for the Library of their Devon house at Saltram (col. pl. 35). Adam was supervising extensive changes at the house. Occasionally Zucchi's detailed bills survive, as for 20 St James's Square, or the one in broken French headed 'Memoire de Mr Zucchi pour des Tableaux peints pour Son Excellence My Lord Mansfield at Kenwood'. They show that, as with most of his fellow craftsmen working on such commissions, he was subject to supervision by Robert Adam. He is perhaps the painter most closely identified with the architect's work.

Giovanni Battista Cipriani (1727–85) came to England in 1755 when the architect William Chambers returned from Italy. Within a year or two he had the honour of decorating George III's State Coach, designed by his new-found architect friend. Adam gave Cipriani the important commission of decorating the ceiling in the Drawing Room at Syon (col. pl. 11).

The drawings reproduced in colour in this book show the areas that a painter usually filled: the centre, as at Mellerstain (col. pl. 39), and often in addition to this circles, rectangles, and lozenges like those in the Harewood ceiling (col. pl. 18). They were usually painted in the studio on paper or canvas cut to the measurements determined on the Adam drawing. We have an example of exactly how Cipriani worked in letters from Sir William Chambers. In 1770, the year of his knighthood, Chambers was retained by the Duke of Bedford to fit up the Library and Dining Room at Woburn. Cipriani, with Biagio Rebecca (1735–1808), provided the paintings, and three extracts from Chambers' letter-book in the British Museum speak for themselves. On 19 May 1770 he wrote that one of the painters would be visiting the house to check the way the light fell on the Library ceiling and to verify some measurements. As the painter spoke no English it was hoped that a member of the family who spoke Italian would help him. On 1 June Chambers indicated that it was necessary to fix up some paper patterns and that a moving scaffold would be needed to reach to the top of the cove. By 22 November he could write that the painters had nearly finished the Library ceiling and that they would soon be visiting Woburn to put up their work. The room was to be cleared for them and moving scaffolds provided for them to stand on.

The subject matter of these squares and roundels was taken from a wide repertory of mythology and ancient history, chosen with due attention to the function of the room: 'Apollo and the Muses' would be put in a Music Room, and poets' or philosophers' heads in the Library, and so forth. On the walls grotesque decoration, which Adam defined in the *Works* as a beautiful light style of ornament used by the ancient Romans, was used. He had seen it in some of the Roman amphitheatres, temples, and tombs, 'the greatest part of which being covered with ruins, have been dug up and cleared by the modern Italians, who for these reasons, give them the name of *grotte*, and hence the word *grotesque*'. But often the large panels were filled with ruin pieces and architectural fantasies (col. pls. 20, 35).

Mr Edward Croft-Murray has carefully listed the painters who worked for Robert Adam.[16] They included Italians, Frenchmen, the occasional Fleming or German, and even a Russian, in company with a sprinkling of native-born

Britons. We have seen that Zucchi was the leader – his work was on Adam's Adelphi house ceiling (col. pl. 36) – but almost in as much demand was Biagio Rebecca, who had arrived in England in 1761, staying until his death in 1808. He worked principally for Adam at Audley End, and for James Wyatt in an Etruscan style at Heaton Hall, near Manchester. The painting of the Adam Etruscan room at Osterley was entrusted to Pietro Maria Borgnis, who trained at the Royal Academy Schools after coming to England with his painter-father Giuseppe Mattia Borgnis. He collaborated on the work of the Etruscan-room ceiling (col. pl. 8) with Zucchi, who painted the centre depicting Hector and Andromache.

A painter of whom we would willingly know more was Michelangelo Pergolesi (fl. 1762–1801). While he is only recorded for the decoration of the sixty-two pilasters in the Long Gallery at Syon (col. pl. 12), he is said to have been sent by Robert Adam from Rome to England, and appears to have become one of his chief assistants. He was the author of *Ornaments and Designs*, of which parts are dedicated to the 1st Lord Scarsdale of Kedleston, the Countess of Buccleuch, and the Duchess of Northumberland, and in which he claimed to have 'long applied his Attention to the Ornaments of the Ancients'.

The native painter used by Adam at Kedleston was William Hamilton (1751–1801), the son of a Scottish assistant to Adam. The architect sent him to Rome, and he studied there under Zucchi, returning to England to enter the Royal Academy Schools. The paintings of Roman ruins in the Saloon at Kedleston were done by him in the late 1760s in oil on canvas (col. pl. 3).

It should be said firmly that Robert Adam was a designer, and that he did not make furniture, fashion silver, weave carpets, or chisel the 'Adam fireplace' of many a saleroom description. It should also be emphasized that cabinet-makers such as Thomas Chippendale, John Linnell, John Cobb, and Ince and Mayhew were capable of realizing their own Neo-Classical ideas in superb furniture without any reference to Adam. There is only, to date, one recorded instance of Chippendale working directly to an Adam design: in the creation of four sofas and eight chairs for the Arlington Street house of Sir Lawrence Dundas. The same is true in the case of John Cobb, whose early Neo-Classical chair of 1764 (pl. 170) – one of a set of eight made for Adam's patron Lord Coventry – shows his complete acceptance of the new mood Adam was doing his utmost to promote, but shows him capable of doing it alone.

In the case of silver and carpets the connexion between architect and craftsman is closer. Thomas Moore of Moorfields, a hosier by trade, but known best as a carpet-maker (and principally for a small group of carpets, of which the Syon Red Drawing Room carpet of 1769 – col. pl. 9 – is perhaps the finest), came into prominence in 1757. In that year he won a Society of Arts premium of £25 for a carpet 'in many respects equal, and in some respects superior to those imported from Persia and Turkey'. He worked at providing carpets for Adam at Croome Court (1768), Syon (1769), Osterley Park (c. 1773), and 20 St James's Square (1774); at St James's Square the design for him to work from was provided by the painter Zucchi, at Syon the design was Pergolesi's.

The Williams-Wynn family, who lived at 20 St James's Square, used Adam to create superb interiors as well as items such as 'Lady William Wynn's Bird Cage' and a grand inkstand for Sir Watkin. The lavish candelabrum by John Carter (pl. 172) would grace their table as similar objects (col. pl. 60) designed by Adam found a place in the homes of many of their contemporaries.

The part played by some architects in designing sculptural monuments, which has long been appreciated, has been brought into clearer focus in recent years by the researches of the late Dr Margaret Whinney, the late Mrs M. I. Webb, and John Physick. In church monuments Adam collaborated with a small group of sculptors, Rysbrack and Peter Vangelder among them, and examples of the realized designs are illustrated here (pls. 173–7). Chimneypieces were obtained from many sources, and towards the end of Adam's life were frequently sent from Italy. The chimneypiece in the Red Drawing Room at Hopetoun House (pl. 28) was executed by Rysbrack in 1756, probably to a design Adam sent from Rome. John Michael Spang provided some chimneypieces at Kedleston, John Hinchcliffe at 20 St James's Square, and so forth – regular employment of a small team of competent sculptors for one of the most important features of any interior.

These chimneypieces were sometimes decorated in ormolu (pl. 159), a material that found many uses in decoration. On 14 August 1770 James Adam wrote to Matthew Boulton, soon to become a principal supplier of ormolu and said by Josiah Wedgwood to be 'the first and most complete manufacturer in England in metal', 'It is desired by Lord Shelburne to send some patterns for chairs or ormolu for the Lamps Mr Boulton is making for Lord Shelburne who spoke much of Mr Boulton's manufacture of ormolu'. James goes on to say that he and his brother Robert 'have long been of opinion that an elegant style in Silver Plate in a manufacture such as Mr Boulton's would take amazingly'. The researches of Mr Nicholas Goodison on Boulton's ormolu manufacture have shown that his work was used in Adam houses, on furniture (pl. 165) and doors (pl. 158).[17] But it was Boulton's own contribution to Neo-Classicism rather than work done to Adam's designs. Indeed, after Lord Shelburne had quarrelled with Adam over the Adelphi Act in 1770 he could still enquire of Boulton in December 1773 'how much these knobs and escutheons finished in your Adam manner will come to per dozen'.

Adam's meticulous attention to detail found its critics: Joseph Gwilt, writing acidly in his *Encyclopedia of Architecture* (1842) of the 'opposite and vile taste of Robert Adam', was neither the first nor last.[18] Sir John Soane, who showed his interest in the Adam style by acquiring about 9,600 of the architect's drawings in 1833, was a calm exception to the general mood.

A firm revival of interest in Adam's work did not really begin until 1867, when Wright and Mansfield, a London firm of cabinet-makers, won the highest honours at the Paris Exhibition for a superb Adam-style cabinet (now in the Victoria & Albert Museum). Publication of selections of plates from the *Works* followed in 1880, 1901, and 1902–3. By the turn of the century, Dr Eileen Harris has noted, 'Everything which had a swag, ram's head, or urns, and was not Chippendale, Sheraton, or Hepplewhite, was Adam'. It was a welcome and merited, if sometimes unthinking, reinstatement of Adam's reputation.

Adam's craftsmen of course had often demonstrated that they had the ability to rise above mere competence to virtuosity. But faced with the new intricacies of Neo-Classicism they might well have been found lacking without careful supervision. Mastery of these intricacies needed a fertile mind, long training, and a touch of daring, all of which, and more – as his surviving work so eloquently testifies – Robert Adam supplied.

Notes

Abbreviation: *RSAJ* for the *Journal* of the Royal Society of Arts.
Unless otherwise given, country of publication is Great Britain.

1   John Summerson, *Architecture in Britain 1530–1830*, 5th revd edn (1969), p. 259.
2   Diocletian's palace at Split, Yugoslavia, is one of the best-preserved of Roman Emperors' palaces.
3   There is a copy in the British Library: it may count as the first important binding in Neo-Classical style (1762).
4   Scottish Record Office, Clerk of Penicuik, MS., 4804. I am indebted to Miss Catherine Cruft for this information.
5   'I saw some months ago, a countryman of yours (Mr. Adam) . . . He seemed to me in one short visit to be a man of genius, and I have heard his knowledge of architecture much applauded'.
6   Ian Bristow, 'Ready-Mixed Paint in the 18th Century', *Architectural Review* 165 (1977), 247–8.
7   Damie Stillman, *The Decorative Work of Robert Adam* (1966), p. 26.
8   Alistair Rowan, 'After the Adelphi: Forgotten Years in the Adam brothers' Practice', *RSAJ*, 122 (1974), 659–78.
9   Rowan, *RSAJ*, 122 (1974), 679–94.
10   John Summerson 'The Master Builders – Adam, all for originality', *Observer* colour supplement (22 August 1976), 27.
11   Fiske Kimball, *Domestic Architecture of the American Colonies and of the Early Republic* (New York, 1966), pp. 110–11, 133–4.
12   'He came at the head of a regiment of artificers': quoted in letter, 20 July 1779, Mrs Montagu to the Duchess of Portland (see p. 23).
13   Geoffrey Beard, *Georgian Craftsmen and their Work* (1966), pp. 72–4.
14   For further lists *see* Geoffrey Beard, *Georgian Craftsmen*, pp. 171–83 and Damie Stillman, *Decorative Work*, pp. 45–50.
15   Beard, *Georgian Craftsmen*, pp. 87–90.
16   Edward Croft-Murray, *Decorative Painting in England 1537–1837* (2 vols., 1962, 1970), vol. 2, pp. 159–305.
17   Nicholas Goodison, *Ormolu, The Work of Matthew Boulton* (1974).
18   A. T. Bolton, 'Robert Adam's Critics', *The Architecture of Robert and James Adam* (2 vols., 1922), vol. 2, pp. 99–114.

BIBLIOGRAPHY

Books

Robert Adam, *Ruins of the Palace of the Emperor Diocletian, at Spalatro, in Dalmatia* (1764). The binding of George III's copy is illustrated here (col. pl. 1).

Robert *and* James Adam, *Works in Architecture* (3 vols., 1773–9; 1822). Reprinted by Thezard, Paris, 1902, by Tiranti 1939, 1959.

Geoffrey Beard, *Georgian Craftsmen and their Work* (1966), *Decorative Plasterwork in Great Britain* (1975).

Arthur T. Bolton, *The Architecture of Robert and James Adam* (2 vols., 1922) – includes a catalogue of the drawings in Sir John Soane's Museum.

H. M. Colvin, *A Biographical Dictionary of British Architects, 1600–1840*, 2nd edn (1978).

Edward Croft-Murray, *Decorative Painting in England, 1537–1837* (2 vols., 1962, 1970) – vol. 2 discusses the painters working for Adam.

J. Mordaunt Crook, *The Greek Revival, Neo-Classical Attitudes in British Architecture, 1760–1870* (1972).

C. P. Curran, *Dublin Decorative Plasterwork of the 17th and 18th Centuries* (1967).

Anthony Dale, *James Wyatt* (1956).

Ralph Edwards *and* Margaret Jourdain, *Georgian Cabinet Makers*, 3rd edn (1962).

John Fleming, *Robert Adam and his Circle in Edinburgh and Rome* (1962).

Gerald K. Geerlings, *Color Schemes of Adam Ceilings* (New York, 1928).

Nicholas P. Goodison, *Ormolu: the Work of Matthew Boulton* (1974).

Eileen Harris, *The Furniture of Robert Adam* (1963).

John Harris, *Sir William Chambers* (1970).

Hugh Honour, *Neo-Classicism* (1968).

Christopher Hussey, *English Country Houses: Mid-Georgian, 1760–1800* (1956).

David Irwin, *English Neo-Classical Art* (1966).

James Lees-Milne, *The Age of Adam* (1947).

James Macaulay, *The Gothic Revival, 1745–1845* (1975).

Mary Mauchline, *Harewood House* (1974).

Clifford Musgrave, *Adam and Hepplewhite . . . Furniture* (1966).

Robert Rowe, *Adam Silver* (1965).

Damie Stillman, *The Decorative Work of Robert Adam* (1967).

John Summerson, *Architecture in Britain, 1530–1830*, 5th edn (1969).

John Swarbrick, *Robert Adam and his Brothers: their Lives, Work and Influence on English Architecture* (1915, reprinted 1959).

H. Avray Tipping, *English Homes, Period VI, 1760–1820* (1926).

Doreen Yarwood, *Robert Adam* (1970).

Articles

Anon., 'Biographical Account of the late Robert Adam Esq., Architect', *Scots Magazine*, 65 (1803), 295–8.

Anon., 'Robert Adam's Drawing Room, No. 4 Royal Terrace, Adelphi', *The Connoisseur*, 141 (1957), 137–9.

Geoffrey Beard, 'Robert Adam at Croome Court', *The Connoisseur*, 132 (1953), 73–6,
    'Robert Adam's Craftsmen', *The Connoisseur Yearbook* (1958), 26–32,
    'A Family's 50-Year Supremacy', *Country Life*, 128 (1960), 1428–9,
    'New Light on Adam's Craftsmen', *Country Life*, 131 (1962), 1098–1100,
    'The Rose family, with a catalogue of their work', *Apollo*, 85 (1967), 266–77.

Arthur T. Bolton, 'Robert Adam as a Bibliographer, Publisher and Designer of Libraries', *Transactions, Bibliographical Society*, 14 (1915–17), 22–30,
    'The Adelphi', *Architectural Review*, 41 (1917), 11–20; 31–5,
    'The Classical and Romantic Compositions of Robert Adam', *Architectural Review*, 57 (1925), 28–34.

Ian Bristow, 'Ready-Mixed Paint in the 18th Century', *Architectural Review*, 161 (1977), 246–8.

Ralph Edwards, 'Torchères and Candelabra by Robert Adam', *Country Life*, 101 (1947), 966–7.

W. R. Eliot, 'The Work of Robert Adam in Northumberland', *Archaeologia Aeliana*, 30 (1952), 106–17.

John Fleming, 'Robert Adam, the Grand-Tourist', *Cornhill Magazine*, 1004 (1955), 118–37,
    'Allan Ramsay and Robert Adam in Italy', *The Connoisseur*, 137 (1956), 79–84,
    'The Journey to Spalatro', *Architectural Review*, 123 (1958), 103–7,
    'Adam Gothic', *The Connoisseur*, 142 (1958), 75–9,
    'Messrs Robert and James Adam: art dealers', *The Connoisseur*, 144 (1959), 168–71,
    'An Italian Sketchbook by Robert Adam, Clérisseau and others', *The Connoisseur*, 146 (1960), 186–94,
    'Robert Adam, Luc-François Breton and the Townshend monument in Westminster Abbey', *The Connoisseur*, 150 (1962), 162–71,
    'Robert Adam's Castle Style', *Country Life*, 143 (1968), 1356–9; 1443–7,
    'A "Retrospective View" by John Clerk of Eldin with some comments on Adam's Castle Style' in *Concerning Architecture: Essays presented to Nikolaus Pevsner*, ed. J. Summerson (1968), 75–84.

Mark Girouard, 'Mellerstain, Berwickshire', *Country Life*, 124 (1958), 416–19; 476–9.

Christopher Gotch, 'Mylne and Adam', *Architectural Review*, 119 (1956), 121–3.

Eileen Harris, 'Robert Adam and the Gobelins', *Apollo*, 81 (1962), 100–16,
    'The Moor Park Tapestries', *Apollo*, 86 (1967), 180–9.

BIBLIOGRAPHY

John Harris, 'The Transparent Portico', *Architectural Review*, 123 (1958), 108–9. (Draws attention to William Talman's anticipation of Adam's portico at Osterley Park in that proposed at Witham Park, Somerset, in the early eighteenth century.)

D. C. Huntington, 'Robert Adam's *Mise-en-Scène* of the human figure', *Journal of the Society of Architectural Historians (of America)*, 27 (1968), 249–63.

Christopher Hussey, 'Farewell Adelphi', *Country Life*, 79 (1936), 161–3.

E. Alfred Jones, 'Adam Silver', *Apollo*, 14 (1939), 55–9.

Fiske Kimball, 'The Moor Park Tapestry Suite of Furniture by Robert Adam', *Philadelphia Museum Bulletin*, 36 (1941), 25–9.

Lesley Lewis, 'Elizabeth Countess of Home and her house in Portman Square', *Burlington Magazine*, 109 (1967), 443–53.

H. M. Nixon, 'An Adam Binding', *Book Collector*, 15 (1966), 184.

Paul Oppé, 'Robert Adam's Picturesque Compositions', *Burlington Magazine*, 80 (1942), 56–9.

James Parker *and* Edith A. Standen, 'The Tapestry Room from Croome Court', in *Decorative Art from the Samuel H. Kress Collection at the Metropolitan Museum of Art* (1964), 2–57. (An expansion of the same authors' article in *Metropolitan Museum of Art Bulletin*, 18 (1959), 76–111, and of those by James Parker in *Antiques*, 77 (1960), 80–2, and *The Connoisseur*, 147 (1961), 109–13.)

W. Rieder, 'Piranesi's *Diverse Maniere*', *Burlington Magazine*, 115 (1973), 308–17.

W. Rieder *and* D. Owsley, 'The Glass Drawing Room from Northumberland House', Victoria and Albert Museum *Yearbook*, 2 (1970), 101–24.

Alistair Rowan, 'Ugbrooke Park, Devon', *Country Life*, 142 (1967), 138–41; 203–7; 266–70,
    'Wedderburn Castle, Berwickshire', *Country Life*, 156 (1974), 345–7,
    'Oxenfoord Castle, Midlothian', *Country Life*, 156 (1974), 430–3,
    'Robert Adam's Last Castles', *Country Life*, 156 (1974), 494–7,
    'After the Adelphi: Forgotten Years in the Adam Brothers' Practice – (i) William Adam and Company, (ii) The Adam Castle Style, (iii) Ideal Villas as Projected and Built', Royal Society of Arts *Journal*, 122 (1974), 659–710,
    'The Royal Society of Arts', *Country Life*, 156 (1974), 1438–41.

Alastair Smart, 'An unknown portrait of James Adam', *Burlington Magazine*, 96 (1954), 101–5.

Robert C. Smith, 'Robert Adam's Drawings for Appleby', *Transactions, Cumberland & Westmorland Architectural Society*, 62 (1962), 305–16.

W. P. D. Stebbing, 'The Adam brothers and their plaster', *Journal, Royal Institute of British Architects*, 45 (1938), 991.

J. Steegman *and* C. K. Adams, 'The Iconography of Robert Adam', *Architectural Review*, 91 (1942), 77–8.

Damie Stillman, 'Robert Adam and Piranesi', in *Essays in the History of Architecture presented to Rudolph Wittkower* (1967), 197–206,
    'The Gallery for Lansdowne House', *Art Bulletin*, 1 (1970), 75–80.

R. W. Symonds, 'Adam and Chippendale: A Myth Exploded', *Country Life Annual* (1958), 53–5.

A. A. Tait, 'The Picturesque Drawings of Robert Adam', *Master Drawings*, 9 (1971), 161–71.

Maurice Tomlin, 'Furniture re-arranged to original designs' [at Osterley], *Country Life*, 167 (1970), 1164–8; 1258–60.

R. B. Wragg, 'Harewood House', *The Archaeological Journal*, 125 (1968), 342–7.

The iconographical problems surrounding Robert Adam (see article by Steegman and Adams, noted above) are further explored in a forthcoming article in the *Burlington Magazine* (July 1978) by Iain G. Brown, 'The Resemblance of a Great Genius: Commemorative Portraits of Robert Adam'.

Catalogues

Iveagh Bequest, Kenwood, *Drawings by R. and J. Adam* (1953).

Newcastle-upon-Tyne, Hatton Art Gallery, *Noble Patronage – The Dukes of Northumberland* (1963).

Iveagh Bequest, Kenwood, *The Adam Style in Furniture* (1964).

Royal Institute of British Architects, *Catalogue of Drawings, A* (1969).

Arts Council of Great Britain for the Council of Europe, *The Age of Neoclassicism* (1972).

Scottish Arts Council, *Robert Adam and Scotland – the Picturesque Drawings* (1972).

Victoria & Albert Museum, *Catalogue of Adam Period Furniture*, ed. Maurice Tomlin (1972).

University of York, King's Manor, *Neo-Classicism in the North* (1975).

During July 1978, the year of publication of this book, three exhibitions are being held in Edinburgh – *Robert Adam at Home* (Scottish Record Office, Register House); *Robert Adam in Italy* (Hopetoun House); and *Scottish Architects at Home and Abroad* (National Library of Scotland). In London in October 1978 an exhibition of watercolours by Robert Adam (and other memorabilia) from Blairadam, selected by Dr A. A. Tait, will be exhibited at the Heinz Gallery of the Royal Institute of British Architects, Drawings Collection. These exhibitions will presumably add to the Adam catalogue literature.

NOTES ON THE PLATES

Portraits, and drawings of Robert Adam's 'Gothic and Italian years' (1749–58), are followed by views of most commissions, arranged in approximate chronological order (it should be remembered that on a number of commissions Adam worked intermittently over a period of years: in all cases the year of Adam's first substantial involvement in a commission is used to establish the chronology). The monochrome section concludes with furnishings, funerary monuments, and a few examples of work inspired by the 'Adam style'. The following colour section includes drawings, views of commissions, furniture, and silver.

Abbreviations in frequent use:

inscr.   inscribed
lit.   books cited. (Bibliographical information is given in full only when the book or article is *not* included in the Bibliography.)
N.M.R.   National Monuments Record, London
S.N.M.R.   Scottish National Monuments Record, Edinburgh
s. & d.   signed and dated

Measurements are metric, height first.

BLACK-AND-WHITE PLATES

Portraits

1 ROBERT ADAM (1728–92). Detail of a portrait attributed to George Willison, *c.* 1773, oil on canvas. *National Portrait Gallery, London* (photograph: Gallery).

For description of portrait *see* No. 5 below.

2 WILLIAM ADAM (1689–1748). Robert Adam's father, portrait attributed to William Aikman, *c.* 1727, oil on canvas, 90 × 70cm. *Keith Adam of Blairadam* (photograph: Scottish National Portrait Gallery).

Aikman's usual price was eight guineas a head.

3 MARY ADAM née Robertson (1699–1761). Robert Adam's mother, portrait by Allan Ramsay, *c.* 1754, oil on canvas, 94 × 71cm. *Yale Center for British Art, Paul Mellon Collection* (photograph: Scottish National Portrait Gallery).

Mary married William Adam in May 1716 and bore him fourteen children: five boys, of whom Robert was the third (William died in infancy), and nine girls.

4 JOHN ADAM (1721–92). Attributed to Francis Cotes, *c.* 1750, oil on canvas, 90 × 71cm. *Keith Adam of Blairadam* (photograph: Scottish National Portrait Gallery).

Both the identity of sitter and artist are uncertain but family tradition regards the portrait as of Robert's elder brother, heir to his father's architectural practice.

5 ROBERT ADAM. Attributed to George Willison, *c.* 1773, oil on canvas, 125 × 105cm. *National Portrait Gallery, London,* no. 2953 (photograph: Gallery).

Willison left for India in 1774, which gives some strength to the supposition that this portrait was painted when the *Works* appeared in 1773 (this is presumably the book on the sitter's knee). The portrait was acquired by Batsford's at Sotheby's on 19 May 1926 (ex Blairadam), and sold to the Gallery in July 1938. The attribution to Willison was strengthened at the time of the Boswell exhibition, 1967, by comparison with Willison's s. & d. portrait of the Douglas claimant.

For detail of head *see* pl. 1.

6 JAMES ADAM (1732–94). By Allan Ramsay, *c.* 1754, oil on canvas, 125 × 105cm. *Laing Art Gallery, Newcastle-upon-Tyne* (photograph: Gallery).

Identified by Professor Alastair Smart (*see* Bibliography). There are preliminary drawings in the National Gallery of Scotland (2022, 2669). The portrait was acquired by Newcastle at Christie's (4 October 1967; G. Baron Ash collection).

7 ROBERT ADAM. Attributed to Laurent Pecheux, *c.* 1755, miniature, gouache on ivory, 11·5 × 8·75cm. *Keith Adam of Blairadam* (photograph: Scottish National Portrait Gallery).

Pecheux was in Rome from 1753 and had many friends in Adam's circle (Fleming, *Robert Adam and his Circle,* p. 352).

8 ROBERT ADAM. Tassie paste medallion, ht 73mm., no inscription, cast in antique form and probably taken about 1792. *Scottish National Portrait Gallery,* no. 201 (photograph: Gallery).

Lit: for this and No. 9 *see* John M. Gray, *James and William Tassie* (1894), nos. 4, 6.

9 ROBERT ADAM. Tassie paste medallion (posthumous), ht 78mm., inscr: 'Robert

Adam/Architect/Died 3 March 1792/In His 64 year'. *Scottish National Portrait Gallery*, no. 262 (photograph: Gallery).

Lit: Gray, op. cit.

10 Detail of Piranesi's dedicatory plate in his *Campus Martius*, with the head of ROBERT ADAM and his own, engraved 1756, published 1762. (Photograph: Stephen Yates.)

While Robert was surprised at Piranesi's flattering dedication, the Italian expected payment for 80 to 100 copies, which Robert, cannily, intended to resell in London (Fleming, *Robert Adam and his Circle*, p. 169). The portrait cannot be relied on in iconographical terms.

Early Drawings

11 A GOTHIC TOWER. Drawing by Robert Adam, s. & d. 1753, inscr: '99', pen, ink, and wash on paper. *Keith Adam of Blairadam* (photograph: Scottish National Portrait Gallery).

12 A GOTHIC CHURCH. Drawing by Robert Adam, s. & d. 1753, inscr: '102', pen, ink, and wash on paper. *Keith Adam of Blairadam* (photograph: Scottish National Portrait Gallery).

13 A GOTHIC FOLLY. Drawing by Robert Adam, s. & d. 1749, pen, ink, and wash on paper. *Keith Adam of Blairadam* (photograph: Scottish National Portrait Gallery).

Presumably made on or after Robert's English tour in 1749.

14 A TEMPLE. Drawing by Robert Adam, s. & d. 1753, inscr: '95', pen, ink, and wash on paper. *Keith Adam of Blairadam* (photograph: Scottish National Portrait Gallery).

15 A FUNERARY MONUMENT. Drawing by Robert Adam, s. & d. 1753, inscr: '96', pen, ink, and wash on paper. *Keith Adam of Blairadam* (photograph: Scottish National Portrait Gallery).

Adam designed some twelve monuments, including one to General Wolfe, which was not executed.

16 A PALACE. Part of a drawing by Robert Adam, Italy *c.* 1756, pen, ink, and wash on paper, length 2·75m. *Sir John Soane's Museum*, vol. 10, no. 1 (photograph: A. C. Cooper).

Fantasies such as this perhaps fevered Robert's imagination to survey actual ruins – Diocletian's palace – and were something of a prelude to James's grand designs for a new Houses of Parliament and a national opera house, 1762–3, which, alas, were never executed.

17 ARCH OF AUGUSTUS at Rimini. Drawing by Charles-Louis Clérisseau, 1755, pen, ink, and wash. *Sir John Clerk Collection* (photograph: Tom Scott).

Robert Adam and Clérisseau went on a sketching expedition together in September 1755 and many drawings by them both survive in the Clerk collection and elsewhere.

18 THE MAUSOLEUM OF THEODORIC at Ravenna. Drawing by Robert Adam, 1755, inscr: '129', pen, ink, and wash. *Sir John Clerk Collection* (photograph: Tom Scott).

Drawn on the autumn expedition with Clérisseau, the mausoleum, erected by Theodoric's daughter in A.D. 528, seems to have been the inspiration for the Auchincruive garden tower (pl. 146) designed by Adam in 1778.

19 HADRIAN'S VILLA near Tivoli. Drawing by Robert Adam, 1756, inscr: '22', pen, ink, and wash. *Keith Adam of Blairadam* (photograph: Scottish National Portrait Gallery).

Robert, Clérisseau, and a young man named Hervey visited Tivoli in April 1756 and 'found the weather so fine and the work so agreeable that we stayed there six days' (Fleming, *Robert Adam and his Circle*, p. 204).

20 Drawing of FALLEN MASONRY. By Robert Adam, *c.* 1756, inscr: '109', pen, ink, and wash. *Sir John Clerk Collection* (photograph: Tom Scott).

The Buildings

21 HOPETOUN HOUSE, West Lothian. Centre of the east front, seen from the south colonnade. 1721– . (Photograph: A. F. Kersting.)

Hopetoun was begun for the 1st Earl of Hopetoun by Sir William Bruce between 1699 and 1703, remodelled across twenty-five years by William Adam, and completed by his sons John and Robert.

22 HOPETOUN HOUSE. The east front, 1721–54. By William, John, and Robert Adam. (Photograph: A. F. Kersting.)

23 HOPETOUN HOUSE. The north pavilion, one of two added to the main block by John and Robert Adam for the 2nd Earl of Hopetoun, 1752–4. (Photograph: A. F. Kersting.)

The most drastic revision of William Adam's original plan was the removal of the central pediment, partly alleviated by the erection of the elegant pavilions.

24–5 HOPETOUN HOUSE. Details of the ceiling plasterwork, Red Drawing Room, *c.* 1754. (Photographs: 24, A. F. Kersting; 25, S.N.M.R.)

The work is attributed to Thomas Clayton, an English worker who settled in Scotland, working extensively for William Adam and his sons.

26 HOPETOUN HOUSE. The Red Drawing Room, *c.* 1754. (Photograph: A. F. Kersting.)

John and Robert Adam provided de-

signs and supervision of the interior decorations for the 2nd Earl of Hopetoun. They introduced the delicate Rococo style, and hoped, in a letter to the Earl (March 1752), that they might 'not despair of pleasing your Lordship as to the lightness of it'.

27 HOPETOUN HOUSE. Detail of the ceiling plasterwork, Yellow Drawing Room, *c.* 1752. (Photograph: S.N.M.R.)

28 HOPETOUN HOUSE. Chimneypiece in the Red Drawing Room, *c.* 1756. (Photograph: S.N.M.R.)

This was provided by the sculptor J. M. Rysbrack to a design possibly sent from Rome by Robert Adam. Rysbrack mentions making it in his letter to Sir Edward Littleton (cited by M. I. Webb, *Michael Rysbrack, Sculptor* (1954), p. 196; *see also* Stillman, *Decorative Work*, p. 89).

29 FORT GEORGE, Inverness-shire. Detail of the fortifications. John and Robert Adam, *c.* 1753. (Photograph: Department of the Environment, Crown Copyright.)

After the '45 rebellion the Board of Ordnance employed William Adam, and later his sons, to construct the Highland forts, of which Fort George is an impressive example. They worked under the superintendence of Colonel William Skinner.

30 FORT GEORGE. The Ravelin Gate. By John and Robert Adam, *c.* 1753. (Photograph: as for No. 29 above.)

This gate has a Vanbrughian grandeur about it, and we must remember not only Adam's admiration for that architect but that Vanbrugh's own work for the Board of Ordnance at Berwick-on-Tweed and elsewhere would be known to him, and to Colonel Skinner.

31 POLLOK HOUSE, Renfrewshire (patron: Sir John Maxwell). Designed by William Adam (d. 1748) and erected by his sons

John and Robert, 1752– . (Photograph: Annan of Glasgow.)

This view shows the house before the addition of wings. It was presented to the City of Glasgow in 1966 and houses part of the Burrell art collections.

32 DUMFRIES HOUSE, Ayrshire (patron: Patrick Crichton, 5th Earl of Dumfries). The main front. Designed by John and Robert Adam, 1754–9. (Photograph: S.N.M.R.)

The foundation stone was laid on 18 June 1754 and the main block was roofed by August 1757. The estimate of £7,971 seems to have been adhered to. The house, illustrated in William Adam's *Vitruvius Scoticus*, pl. 20 (issued posthumously as late as 1810), contains superb Chippendale furniture delivered in 1759.

33 HATCHLANDS, Surrey (patron: Admiral the Hon. Edward Boscawen). The west front, *c.* 1758. (Photograph: A. F. Kersting.)

One of the first houses at which Adam worked on his return from Italy. He was not responsible for the main structure, which has been attributed to Thomas Ripley (d. 1758), but provided important plastered interiors.

34 HATCHLANDS. Detail of the Library Room ceiling, *c.* 1759. (Photograph: the National Trust.)

It has been shown that Adam turned for the source of this early decoration to details of the seventeenth-century dome at the Villa Pamphili in Rome. The relevant drawings are reproduced by Stillman (*Decorative Work*, pls. 117–19). Adam added allusions to his client's connexion with the sea.

35 HATCHLANDS. Detail of the Dining Room ceiling, *c.* 1759. (Photograph: *Country Life*.)

The surrender of Louisburg in 1758 by the French to the British Navy and Army

under Boscawen of Hatchlands and Amherst brought Adam's patron the thanks of Parliament. The plasterwork by an unknown worker makes playful allusions to the Admiral's nautical interests (*see also* pl. 34).

36 SHARDELOES, Buckinghamshire (patron: William Drake). The east front, 1759–61. (Photograph: A. F. Kersting.)

A drawing in the Soane Museum of May 1759 (vol. 31, no. 97) is covered with pencilled alterations (the handsome portico with its fine Corinthian columns is one such alteration) and may indicate that Adam did what he was often to do throughout his life – to take over a scheme from another architect and to design the interiors. The house was extensively remodelled to high standards in 1960.

37 SHARDELOES. Detail of the Hall ceiling, 1761–3; plasterwork: Joseph Rose & Company. (Photograph: A. F. Kersting.)

Rose's plasterwork at the house (charged for between October 1761 and February 1763, Bucks. Co. Record Office, Shardeloes MSS.) closely followed the Adam designs. The Hall ceiling drawing (Soane Museum, vol. 11, no. 63) was used again with modifications at Syon.

38 CROOME COURT, Worcestershire (patron: George William, 6th Earl of Coventry). Drawing inscr: 'Cieling for the Library at Croome', and dated 'Janry 1763' (Soane Museum, vol. 11, no. 37). Plasterer: Joseph Rose & Company. (Photograph: Metropolitan Museum of Art, New York.)

The ceiling was designed for the Library but erected in the Tapestry Room (pl. 39).

39 CROOME COURT. Ceiling of the Tapestry Room, *c.* 1763. (Photograph: Metropolitan Museum of Art, New York.)

The ceiling was executed by Joseph Rose with hardly any change from the drawing (pl. 38). The Tapestry Room was moved to New York and erected at the Metropolitan Museum as the gift of the Kress Foundation (1958–9).

40 CROOME COURT. The Gallery (originally Library), 1761–6. (Photograph: N.M.R.)

In March 1761 Adam submitted a second design for the Gallery ceiling (Soane Museum, vol. 11, nos. 34, 36), which Lord Coventry accepted. Adam then modified the design for the room in June 1763 to include the statues and bas-reliefs. Joseph Rose did the plasterwork in 1764 and Joseph Wilton charged £300 for the chimneypiece in 1766, the date of the grisaille painting above it.

41 CROOME COURT. The Garden Temple, c. 1765. (Photograph: N.M.R.)

Adam commenced work at Croome in 1760 – the house itself was designed by 'Capability' Brown – and as well as important interiors he designed or altered many garden buildings, including this circular temple.

CROOME COURT: *see also* col. pl. 2.

42 WHITEHALL, London. The Admiralty Screen, 1760–1. Published in the *Works*, 1775. Inscr. (in English and French): 'View of Part of Whitehall, Shewing the Admiralty office, with the new Gateway designed & executed in the year 1760'. (Photograph: Joe Thompson.)

The Screen was altered in 1827 and has since been restored.

43 KEDLESTON, Derbyshire (patron: Sir Nathaniel Curzon, Bt, created Lord Scarsdale April 1761). Painting, oil on canvas, c. 1765. The north front of the house, with bridge and garden buildings. *The Viscountess Scarsdale* (photograph: *Country Life*).

44 KEDLESTON. The south front, 1760–5. (Photograph: A. F. Kersting.)

The first architect used by Sir Nathaniel Curzon was Matthew Brettingham. James Paine also made plans, which seem to have been carried out as far as foundation levels. Their places were taken by Adam, who designed the south front in Roman style. It bears a final date of 1765 cut on a panel between the central figures above the entrance.

45 KEDLESTON. Design for the Library, 1768. *Sir John Soane's Museum*, vol. 14, no. 122 (photograph: A. C. Cooper).

One of the many designs that does not seem to have been executed, the drawing shows Adam's attempts at proportion and elegant decoration. The bookcases on the left are to hold books on 'Ancient History', those on the right 'Modern History'. The decoration is similar to that Adam proposed for the painted Breakfast Room (Soane Museum, vol. 14, no. 125), also of 1768.

46 KEDLESTON. Hall, chimneypiece on west wall *c*. 1765. (Photograph: A. F. Kersting.)

The imposing hall at Kedleston with its Derbyshire alabaster columns was a long time in its evolution under Brettingham, Paine, and Adam, but was largely complete by 1765. Adam's only dated drawing for the Hall (Soane Museum, vol. 40, no. 3) is of 1761. George Richardson was responsible for the ceiling and Joseph Rose charged £29 0s. 6d. (Kedleston MSS., 3R.f64) for the attractive plasterwork over the chimneypiece.

47 KEDLESTON. The Dining Room, begun 1760. (Photograph: A. F. Kersting.)

The 1760–1 dated drawings for the walls, chimneypiece, and ceiling (Soane Museum, vol. 22, no. 16; vol. 11, no. 53; vol. 40, nos. 20–3) show that the room was executed more or less as designed. The plasterer was Joseph Rose (£270 3s. 3½d.), and the chimneypiece one of four provided by Michael Spang (d. 1762). The paintings are attributed as follows: four roundels to Antonio Zucchi; oblong panels to William Hamilton; and the central roundel to Henry Morland.

KEDLESTON: *see also* col. pl. 3.

48 THE SHAMBLES AND BUTTER MARKET, High Wycombe, Buckinghamshire, 1761 (patron: the 'Mayor and Council of High Wycombe'). (Photograph: High Wycombe Public Library.)

Adam rebuilt this building in 1761, but the present lantern was added *c.* 1900.

49 COMPTON VERNEY, Warwickshire (patron: Lord Willoughby de Broke). The wings and portico, *c.* 1765. (Photograph: Michael Felmingham.)

Adam designed a number of features at this Vanbrugh-type house, including forward projecting wings, an orangery, and a bridge, and carried out some interior remodelling.

50 BOWOOD, Wiltshire (patron: John, Earl of Shelburne). The south portico, altered by Robert Adam, 1763, as part of his task in amending work of 1755–60 by Henry Keene. (Photograph: A. F. Kersting.)

The 'Big House' by Keene was demolished and the contents and ceilings dispersed by sale on 30 June 1955. Bolton (*Architecture*, vol. 1, p. 215) cites a note in the Bowood archives: '8th October 1763. The Portico is almost finished . . . to altering ten Colloms and new Bases at South Portico as agreed with Mr Adams . . . £35'.

51 BOWOOD. Detail of the arabesque plaster panel in the Dining Room, *c.* 1763. (Photograph: A. F. Kersting.)

This panel, with variations, appears in many houses, and may be regarded as an effective part of typical Adam decoration.

52 BOWOOD. Ceiling of the 'King's Room', *c.* 1763. (Photograph: A. F. Kersting.)

This ceiling (8·9 × 6·1m.) was lot 204 in the sale of 30 June 1955 and was then unsold. The plasterer was Joseph Rose junior (pl. 108): a notable example of his work at Bowood was removed and installed in 1956, with minor alterations, at Lloyd's of London.

53 BOWOOD. Entrance Hall, detail of the balcony, *c.* 1768. (Photograph: A. F. Kersting.)

The carved work at Bowood is attributed to John Gilbert, who was employed at Lord Shelburne's London house. This Bowood work was dispersed when Henry Keene's 'Big House' was demolished in 1956.

54 BOWOOD. The 'Diocletian' wing from the roof of the 'Big House', 1769–70. (Photograph: N.M.R.)

In a picturesque way the 'Diocletian' wing can be likened to the Emperor's palace at Spalato; the impressionable patron acquired in addition to a hint of Antiquity an interesting range of proportioned buildings. The garden layout was designed by Sir Charles Barry in the 1840s.

55 BOWOOD. The Mausoleum, 1761–3, for the Countess of Shelburne. (Photograph: N.M.R.)

When Lord Shelburne died on 10 May 1761 his widow seems to have asked Adam to design a mausoleum with catacombs beneath. His plan and elevations (Soane Museum, vol. 39, nos. 75–80) are of 1761; the mason John Button had completed the building by 1763.

56 OSTERLEY PARK, Middlesex (patron: Francis Child, 1735–63). The portico, *c.* 1762. (Photograph: A. F. Kersting.)

Horace Walpole wrote of Osterley to the Countess of Upper Ossory on 21 June 1773: 'there is a double portico that fills the space between the towers of the front and is as noble as the Propyleum of Athens'.

The important influence on the design of the Osterley portico (noted by John Harris) was William Talman's work in the early eighteenth century at Witham Park, Somerset, which Robert Adam visited in connexion with work he was doing there in 1762. Work at Osterley after 1763 was done for Francis Child's brother, Robert.

57 OSTERLEY PARK. View from the inner courtyard looking outwards through the portico. (Photograph: A. F. Kersting.)

This podium level is reached from the approach side by ascending twenty steps and passing through the great atrium of columns that connects the forward brick wings of the house.

58 OSTERLEY PARK. The soffit of the portico. (Photograph: N.M.R.)

The ceiling, with its dominant central octagon, bears some resemblance to that in the Hall at Shardeloes (pl. 37).

59 OSTERLEY PARK. The Entrance Hall, 1767–8. (Photograph: Victoria & Albert Museum, hereafter 'V. & A. Museum'.)

The decoration of this room was a successful synthesis of the flat and linear motifs. There is a careful pattern relationship between ceiling and inlaid floor, the focal points of apse and wall panels, and the delicate blue and white colouring. The many drawings for the room are discussed by Stillman (*Decorative Work*, p. 69).

60 OSTERLEY PARK. Drawing, s. & d. 1767, for the Entrance Hall ceiling. *V. & A. Museum* (photograph: Museum).

This drawing differs slightly in the outer panels from that in the Soane Museum (vol. 11, no. 203), and from the ceiling as executed (pl. 59).

61 OSTERLEY PARK. Detail of plaster

trophy panel in the Entrance Hall, 1767. (Photograph: V. & A. Museum.)

Adam used these Roman-inspired trophies, based on those on the Campidoglio in Rome – the Trophies of Marius – at both Syon (col. pl. 15) and Osterley. He possessed large wash drawings of the originals (Soane Museum, vol. 26, nos. 89–92; Stillman, *Decorative Work*, p. 64). At both Osterley and Syon the trophies were executed by Joseph Rose & Company.

62 OSTERLEY PARK. One of the three glass and ormolu lanterns (pl. 63), *c.* 1770. Ht 86·5cm. (Photograph: V. & A. Museum.)

A sketch for the lanterns is in the Soane Museum (vol. 6, no. 60) and one is reproduced in the *Works* (vol. 3, pl. 8), wrongly described as 'Furniture at Sionhouse'.

63 OSTERLEY PARK. The staircase, 1768. (Photograph: V. & A. Museum.)

A precise blend of Corinthian columns and pilasters matching the upward sweep of the staircase. The metal balusters of many of Adam's staircases were provided by Thomas Tilston: as well as those at Osterley there are good examples at Newby (pl. 106) and 20 St James's Square. The three lanterns were listed in the 1782 inventory as 'Three elegant lamps mounted in Or Molee'.

64 OSTERLEY PARK. Detail, centre panel of Drawing Room chimneypiece, *c.* 1772. (Photograph: V. & A. Museum.)

It is not possible, in the absence of documentation, to be certain of the date of an actual chimneypiece, as opposed to the date of the room in which it was inserted. We know that this room was completed by the summer of 1773, when Horace Walpole first visited the house. The chimneypieces at Osterley are attributed to Joseph Wilton (1722–1803, one of the founder members of the Royal Academy) on the basis of one in the Gallery there, which is close to designs by Sir William Chambers.

65 OSTERLEY PARK. Detail of door architrave, Drawing Room, *c.* 1772. (Photograph: V. & A. Museum.)

The ram's head was a favourite Neo-Classical motif. Here it terminates the two console brackets at the top corners of the door architrave.

66 OSTERLEY PARK. Design for the Drawing Room carpet, *c.* 1773. *V. & A. Museum* (photograph: Museum).

This drawing is similar to that in the Soane Museum (vol. 17, no. 186), and the carpet weaver followed it almost exactly. The carpets could make an important contribution to unifying the room with the other elements of the decoration. Adam therefore relied on Thomas Moore of London and Thomas Whitty of Axminster to provide carpets to his designs.

67 OSTERLEY PARK. Detail of the Drawing Room carpet, *c.* 1773. (Photograph: V. & A. Museum.)

The reliable attribution of this carpet on the evidence of manufacturing techniques is to Thomas Moore of Moorfields, who was awarded a premium in 1756 for the excellence of his work. His most famous carpet is that of *c.* 1769 in the Red Drawing Room at Syon (col. pl. 9).

Lit: Wendy Hefford, 'Thomas Moore of Moorfields', *The Burlington Magazine*, 119 (1977), 840–7.

68 OSTERLEY PARK. The Library, 1766–73. (Photograph: A. F. Kersting.)

This room – the first designs for which are dated 1766 – was completed by 1773. The inset paintings are by Zucchi, except for the two over the fireplaces, which are attributed to Cipriani. The furniture was provided by John Linnell about 1770, and includes a pedestal desk, veneered with stained sycamore, and the lyre-back chairs.

The bookcases are almost certainly the work of John Gilbert, whose name appears regularly in Adam's bank account from the opening entry in 1764.

69 OSTERLEY PARK. Detail of chimneypiece, Etruscan Dressing Room, *c.* 1777. (Photograph: V. & A. Museum.)

The fan and palmette are motifs found frequently in Neo-Classical decoration, and were particularly used on door architraves and the friezes of chimneypieces.

70 OSTERLEY PARK. Door in the Etruscan Dressing Room, *c.* 1776. (Photograph: V. & A. Museum.)

This door, one of two in the room, has six painted panels, presumably by Pietro Maria Borgnis, who painted the walls and the ceiling (except for the central roundel, which is by Antonio Zucchi).

71 OSTERLEY PARK. Detail of the centre right panel of the Etruscan Dressing Room door (pl. 70). (Photograph: V. & A. Museum.)

72 GIOVANNI BATTISTA PIRANESI (1720–78). Detail of design for a chimneypiece and wall, from his *Diverse Maniere D' Adornare I Cammini* (1769, pl. 2). (Photograph: Joe Thompson.)

Adam seems to have taken his inspiration for the decoration of the Etruscan Dressing Room at Osterley both from Classical urns and vases, as he acknowledges in the *Works* (vol. 2, pt 1), and from the designs for chimneypieces published by his erstwhile friend Piranesi. There is 'a similarity of general conception and scale' between the Piranesi drawing and the room itself (Stillman, *Decorative Work*, p. 76).

Lit: Rieder, 'Piranesi's *Diverse Maniere*'.

73 OSTERLEY PARK. Preliminary design for wall decoration, Etruscan Dressing Room, *c.* 1775. *V. & A. Museum, Dept of*

Prints and Drawings, no. 3436–41 (photograph: Museum).

The actual wall decoration was varied by the substitution of painted dancing maidens and the omission of the ovals surmounting the tripod pedestals.

74 OSTERLEY PARK. Drawing of 2 June 1777, inscr: 'Chimney board for the Etruscan Dressing Room at Osterly'. *Sir John Soane's Museum*, vol. 17, no. 137 (photograph: V. & A. Museum).

The chimneyboard, a fine composition of painted canvas with a wooden frame and brass handle, is still in the Etruscan Dressing Room.

Lit: Tomlin, V. & A. *Catalogue*, 79.

75 OSTERLEY PARK. Chimneyboard for the State Bedroom, painted canvas on wooden frame, brass handle, 1778. Ht 117cm. (Photograph: V. & A. Museum.)

These elegant pieces of mounted canvas effectively stopped draughts from the chimney; Adam provided them in the State Bedroom and the Etruscan Dressing Room (pl. 74). His design for the State Bedroom chimneyboard (Soane Museum, vol. 17, no. 138) is dated 22 August 1778.

76–7 OSTERLEY PARK. Details of the statuary marble chimneypiece, State Bedroom, *c.* 1777. (Photograph: V. & A. Museum.)

Pl. 77 shows the top left corner of the chimneypiece and pl. 76 the centre panel. (*See also* pl. 64.)

78 OSTERLEY PARK. Ceiling of the Etruscan Grotto, 1779. (Photograph: V. & A. Museum.)

This is an excellent example of the precise symmetry of Neo-Classical decoration, and represents almost the last work Adam and Rose did at Osterley. The ceiling was reconstructed in 1950 by G. Jackson & Sons to the original design.

OSTERLEY PARK: *see also* col. pls. 4–8.

79 SYON HOUSE, Brentwood, Middlesex (patron: 1st Duke of Northumberland). The west front, remodelled by Adam (but see below). (Photograph: A. F. Kersting.)

Adam did a great deal of work and submitted many plans in an attempt to modernize the buildings of the medieval convent at Syon. The present external appearance, however, owes something to work, including casing in Bath stone, done about 1825, probably by Charles Fowler.

80 SYON HOUSE. Dining Room, detail of the domed ceiling in the apse, *c.* 1764. (Photograph: A. F. Kersting.)

Rose has here worked to an Adam design (Soane Museum, vol. 11, nos. 16, 18) that incorporates an intricate low-relief pattern, refined and inventive.

81 SYON HOUSE. Drawing Room, detail of the ceiling, *c.* 1766. (Photograph: N.M.R.)

This room has extremely delicate fan-work in plaster, with inserted paintings, probably by Francesco Zuccarelli (1702–88), who did some work in the Long Gallery at Syon (col. pl. 13; pl. 82).

82 SYON HOUSE. Long Gallery, detail of the centre of the ceiling, *c.* 1766. (Photograph: A. F. Kersting.)

Adam had made designs for the ceiling in August 1761 and (as executed) in August 1763 (Soane Museum, vol. 11, nos. 22–3). Space was allowed in Joseph Rose's plasterwork to incorporate paintings, which are probably by Francesco Zuccarelli. For details of documentation *see* Beard, *Georgian Craftsmen*, p. 81; Stillman, *Decorative Work*, p. 64.

83 SYON HOUSE. Entrance Hall, *c.* 1761–. (Photograph: A. F. Kersting.)

A room in grand Roman manner, 22 × 10 × 11m., executed almost as designed (Soane Museum, vol. 39, no. 37). Curved stairs flank the *Dying Gaul* and lead to the Ante-Room (col. pl. 15). The plasterwork, by Joseph Rose & Company, is in the heavy style of the early Adam works (*see* pl. 40), with effective use of the Doric order in the screen and walls. The height of the room (11m.) was made possible by rationalizing different levels in the medieval building.

84 SYON HOUSE. The Dining Room, *c.* 1761–9. (Photograph: A. F. Kersting.)

Each end of this imposing room has an apse (for ceiling *see* pl. 80) supported by Corinthian columns. The room was designed in 1761, and, apart from the grisaille panels over the niches, which Andrea Casali provided in 1769, was completed in 1767.

85 SYON HOUSE. Detail of Long Gallery, 1766–8, showing portrait of Adam's patron, the 1st Duke of Northumberland. (Photograph: N.M.R.)

The portrait, loosely after Gainsborough's portrait at Alnwick, is flanked by two of the sixty-two pilasters decorated by Pergolesi (*see* col. pls. 12–14).

86 SYON HOUSE. Engraving from the *Works* (vol. 1, pt 1, pl. 4). Perspective view of the Bridge (1768). (Photograph: Joe Thompson.)

This attractive Neo-Classical bridge was not built. It was intended to have arch spans of 7m. in the centre and two at 4·75m., and to be placed over the river in the grounds at Syon. The Adam drawing is in the Soane Museum (vol. 51, no. 10).

87 SYON HOUSE. Entrance gateway and screen, *c.* 1773. (Photograph: A. F. Kersting.)

Horace Walpole, writing to the Revd William Mason on 29 July 1773, said of this gateway and screen: 'it is all lace and embroidery, and as *croquant* as his frames for tables; consequently most improper to be exposed in the high road to Brentford'. Modern planners have disturbed its symmetry with the injudicious siting of a lamp-post. The Adam drawing is in the Soane Museum (vol. 51, no. 94).

SYON HOUSE: *see also* col. pls. 9–15.

88 An illuminated TRANSPARENCY for Queen Charlotte 'in Honour of His Majesty's Birthday', June 1763. From the *Works* (vol. 1, pt 1, pl. 5). (Photograph: Joe Thompson.)

The structure was erected in the garden at old Buckingham House, with the intention that the King should see the transparency at night – an effective piece of stage carpentry enhanced by patron, architect, and the identity of the 'recipient'.

89 MERSHAM LE HATCH, Kent (patron: Sir Edward Knatchbull, Bt). The south front, 1762–5. (Photograph: N.M.R.)

A tablet in the house records that Thomas Cole, builder, worked to Adam's designs: the foundation stone was laid on 13 September 1762 and the house was roofed by 26 September 1765. Tradition confidently asserts the use of three million bricks.

90 MERSHAM LE HATCH. Drawing Room ceiling, centre panel, 1766. (Photograph: N.M.R.)

Adam provided a design in 1766 (Soane Museum, vol. 11, no. 182), which was executed by Joseph Rose & Company. It is an intricate pattern, with prominence given to the central motif surrounded by panels of curving rinceau.

91 CROOME D'ABITOT, Worcestershire. Detail of Gothic pulpit tester, Croome church, *c.* 1763. (Photograph: N.M.R.)

'Capability' Brown designed the church at Croome for the 6th Earl of Coventry, but the interior Gothic fittings were done by Robert Adam (drawings: Soane Museum, vol. 50, nos. 15–21), and included font, Gothic chairs, ceiling, the iron gate, and cusping to the arches and wall tablets.

92 UGBROOKE PARK, Devon (patron: 4th Lord Clifford). The south and west fronts, 1764–8. (Photograph: *Country Life*.)

A house in 'toy-fort' style: a square range of buildings with corner towers surrounding a yard. At the right is a wing (incorporating part of the old house and a Catholic chapel) in which the family lived while the new house was being built. It is the first Adam castle.

Lit: Rowan, 'Ugbrooke Park'.

93 HAREWOOD HOUSE, Yorkshire (patron: Edwin Lascelles, Earl of Harewood). Drawing, 1771, inscr: '2d. Design of a Chimney Piece for the Gallery at Harewood'. *Sir John Soane's Museum* (photograph: N.M.R.).

The Soane collection of drawings (vol. 22) contains twenty-seven of chimneypieces for Harewood. Many were not executed, or were moved during the remodelling of the house in the 1840s by Sir Charles Barry. Those relating to the Gallery (nos. 199–206) are dated between 1771 and 1774.

94 HAREWOOD HOUSE. The Entrance Hall, *c.* 1765–7. (Photograph: A. F. Kersting.)

The Adam drawings for the interior of Harewood are mostly dated 1765, the year in which Lascelles returned from Paris. The Hall is unusual, with bold engaged columns in place of pilasters, and with arches and bas-relief panels. Joseph Rose included the Hall in his plasterwork account of 1766–70 at a charge of £333. Some of the panels were, however, executed by William Collins (*see* No. 95).

95 HAREWOOD HOUSE. The Library chimneypiece, *c.* 1769. (Photograph: A. F. Kersting.)

John Devall, the King's Master Mason, provided most of the chimneypieces at Harewood, but the overmantel panel, representing a pagan sacrifice (there is a matching chimneypiece on the other side of the room with a panel depicting Bacchic revellers), was provided by William Collins (1721–93), a London specialist in such decorative niceties.

96 HAREWOOD HOUSE. Drawing, elevation of the south front, *c.* 1761, inscr: 'South Front of a *NEW DESIGN* for GAWTHORP HOUSE in *YORKSHIRE* the Seat of Edwin Lascelles Esquire'. Signed: 'Ro. Adam, Architect'. *Sir John Soane's Museum*, vol. 35, no. 6 (photograph: R. B. Fleming & Company).

Adam obviously supplied Lascelles with many ideas for Harewood, of which this is one, but the main work of construction was entrusted to John Carr – the Adam state rooms date from 1765 – and the exterior was in any case altered by Sir Charles Barry in the 1840s.

97 HAREWOOD HOUSE. Drawing of the Library, 1765, inscr: 'Design for finishing the Library at Gawthorp House in Yorkshire. The Seat of Edwin Lascelles Esquire'. *Sir John Soane's Museum*, vol. 35, no. 15 (photograph: N.M.R.).

Lascelles accepted this second design; and the room still resembles the original conception. The paintings are by Biagio Rebecca, on the theme of 'The Education of Pliny's Daughter'.

HAREWOOD HOUSE: *see also* col. pls. 18–21.

98 KIMBOLTON CASTLE, Huntingdonshire (patron: 4th Duke of Manchester). The Gate House, *c.* 1765. (Photograph: *Country Life*.)

Adam was here providing an appropriate entrance to Vanbrugh's great house at Kimbolton (1706–9), and using the Doric order to effect. His five designs are in the

Soane Museum (vol. 30, nos. 143–5; vol. 51, nos. 87–8).

99 STRAWBERRY HILL, Middlesex (patron: Horace Walpole). Chimneypiece in the Round Drawing Room, c. 1766. (Photograph: *Country Life*.)

There are two Adam designs for chimneypieces for Horace Walpole (Soane Museum, vol. 22, nos. 227–8). The one executed, which follows the drawing closely, has scagliola inlays. Walpole wrote to George Montagu on 31 March 1770 that, after a delay of five years 'standing still', the room was nearing completion (*see* Bolton, *Architecture*, vol. 1, p. 91).

100 NOSTELL PRIORY, Yorkshire (patron: Sir Rowland Winn). Drawing, c. 1767, inscr: 'Design of a Cieling for the Saloon at Nostel. The Seat of Sir Rowland Wynn Baronet'. *Nostell Archives* (photograph: Stephen Yates).

This design was not executed, but it shows the problem of relating the decoration on the deep cove of the room with that at the centre of the ceiling. The state rooms at Nostell were laid out with Rococo plasterwork, in the 1740s, by James Paine. In some cases Adam blended his own work with Paine's, in others he supplanted it by overall treatment.

101 NOSTELL PRIORY. The Library, 1766–7. (Photograph: A. F. Kersting.)

The first room in the house to be remodelled by Adam for the 5th baronet, the Library is the best preserved of his Nostell interiors. The room's unity was achieved by careful juxtaposition of the work of the best craftsmen – paintings by Zucchi, plasterwork by Rose, and furniture by Chippendale. The superb desk in the foreground was provided by Chippendale in 1767 at a cost of £72 10s.; it is also shown in the portrait of Sir Rowland and Lady Winn that stands on an easel near it.

NOSTELL PRIORY: *see also* col. pls. 22–4.

102 NEWBY HALL, Yorkshire (patron: William Weddell). The south front, c. 1705, with the two-storey Adam wing attached c. 1767–76. (Photograph: N.M.R.)

The main building was done for Sir William Blackett (d. 1713); Adam was called in by William Weddell (whose father had purchased the estate from John Blackett) to decorate the main rooms and provide a sculpture gallery (col. pl. 33; pl. 104).

103 NEWBY HALL. Detail of the Library chimneypiece, statuary marble, c. 1770. (Photograph: A. F. Kersting.)

Most of the decorative elements of the Neo-Classical style are seen to advantage on chimneypieces and door-cases – the urns, the paterae, the flowing rinceau on the central tablet, and the stylized, enigmatic faces of gods and goddesses were popular with architect and patron alike.

104 NEWBY HALL. Drawing, section of the Sculpture Gallery, c. 1767. Inscr: 'Section of a Room for the Reception of Antique Statues Bas reliefs Busts and Sarcophagi & c. for William Weddell Esquire, at Newby near Boroughbridge, Yorkshire'. *Mr & Mrs Robin Compton* (photograph: A. F. Kersting).

For a note on the Sculpture Gallery *see* that to col. pl. 33.

105 NEWBY HALL. Drawing, the Library ceiling, s. & d. 'Robt Adam, Architect 1767'. *Mr & Mrs Robin Compton* (photograph: A. F. Kersting).

This fine drawing shows the ceiling more or less as executed. The centre medallion contains a painting by Zucchi (cols. pls. 27–8) set within the oval.

106 NEWBY HALL. Staircase Hall, c. 1768. (Photograph: *Country Life*.)

The staircase shows the elegant metal balusters commonly supplied by the London smith Thomas Tilston, a craftsman, it seems, of Welsh origin, who worked at Eaton Hall, Cheshire, in the 1730s. He is documented as having provided the staircase at 20 St James's Square, and probably supplied that at Osterley (pl. 63).

Newby Hall: *see also* col. pls. 27–33.

107 Kenwood, Middlesex (patron: William Murray, 1st Earl of Mansfield). The portico on the north front, *c.* 1769–70. (Photograph: A. F. Kersting.)

This feature with its composite columns remains almost as Adam designed it, but the wings at each side were added by George Saunders, a follower of the architect Henry Holland, in 1793–6.

108 Joseph Rose junior (1745–99). Self-portrait in crayons, 60·9×45·7cm. *Sir Richard Sykes, Bt, Sledmere, Yorkshire* (photograph: Warren Jepson, Leeds).

The portrait was subsequently engraved by Bartolozzi with the inscription: 'Joseph Rose Esqr. ob. Feb 11 1799. Ætatis Suae 53. From a drawing in Crayons by himself'.

Rose assisted Sir Christopher Sykes in designing the decorative work at Sledmere (1788–90), and two volumes of his sketches are preserved in the house. He, and his uncle Joseph (*c.* 1723–80), were responsible for plasterwork at almost every Adam commission.

109 Kenwood. Detail of Joseph Rose junior's gilded plasterwork, apse ceiling of the Library, 1769. (Photograph: Greater London Council, the Iveagh Bequest.)

110 Kenwood. Design of the Library ceiling, 1767, published in the *Works* (vol. 1, pt 2, pl. 7). (Photograph: Joe Thompson.)

The final ceiling was a collaboration between Joseph Rose junior as the plasterer and Antonio Zucchi as the decorative painter (*see* col. pl. 34). The Adam drawings are in the Soane Museum (vol. 11,

nos. 111–12) and the actual work is closely modelled on them. Zucchi charged for his paintings in 1769.

Kenwood: *see also* col. pl. 34.

111 Saltram, Devon (patron: John Parker). The Saloon, 1768–9. (Photograph: A. F. Kersting.)

This 'Great Room' as it is called in the Saltram accounts still has its original Axminster carpet designed by Adam (Soane Museum, vol. 17, no. 178) and delivered in 1770 by Thomas Whitty (£126). The chimneypiece is attributed to Thomas Carter the younger. The ceiling incorporates nine oil-on-paper roundels of mythological subjects painted in 1769 by Antonio Zucchi and referred to in a letter from Mrs Parker to her brother. The pair of chandeliers, of early-nineteenth-century date, seem a little too heavy in style for the room.

Saltram: *see also* col. pl. 35.

112 The Adelphi, London. 'Society for the Encouragement of Arts, Manufactures & Commerce . . . in John Street' (later Royal Society of Arts). Elevation of principal front, from the *Works* (vol. 1, pt 2, pl. 4). (Photograph: Joe Thompson.)

Adam entered into an agreement with the Society on 21 March 1772 to erect a suitable house for it in the Adelphi, which the Society would then lease from him from June 1774 onwards. The exterior of the building survives almost as erected, and was spared in the 1936 demolition of the Adelphi (pl. 113).

113 The Adelphi. The Royal Society of Arts, 1772–4. Photographed as work was in progress on the demolition of the Adelphi scheme in 1936. (Photograph: A. F. Kersting.)

114 The Adelphi. Royal Terrace, photographed *c.* 1930. (Photograph: N.M.R.)

Adam, David Garrick, Dr James Graham, and the Hon. Topham Beauclerk all lived in the Royal Terrace. The Terrace was demolished in 1936 but the ceiling from Garrick's house (like that from Adam's house, No. 4) was saved, and is re-erected in the V. & A. Museum (drawing: col. pl. 37).

115 THE ADELPHI. The arches, *c.* 1768, looking up Lower Adam Street. (Photograph: N.M.R.)

The massive brick arches were built to support terraces of houses and to provide access roads in the lower levels of the scheme (for plan *see* Bolton, *Architecture*, vol. 2, pp. 24–6). Flooding from the Thames was frequent owing to the base level being some 60cm. too low.

116 THE ADELPHI. Detail of ceiling in No. 4 Royal Terrace, *c.* 1772. (Photograph: A. F. Kersting.)

This was Adam's own house in the Royal Terrace, which he lived in from 1772 to 1786; although it was demolished with the rest of the great Adelphi scheme in 1936, the inset paintings were saved (the central one by Zucchi is shown in col. pl. 36).

THE ADELPHI: *see also* col. pls. 36–7.

117 GUNTON CHURCH (St Andrew), North Walsham, Norfolk, 1769 (patron: Sir William Harbord). (Photograph: N.M.R.)

This church with its fine four-column portico stands some 70m. from Gunton Park, which James Wyatt embellished for the same patron in 1785. It is very much like a small garden temple; it has a circular vestibule and coved ceiling with a fine plaster frieze.

118 PULTENEY BRIDGE, Bath, Somerset, 1769–74. Aquatint by Thomas Malton, 1788, 32×47cm. (Photograph: N.M.R.)

To connect Bath to his private estate

William Pulteney employed Adam, a good friend, to design this bridge. The builder, Reed, was finally ruined by the undertaking. Rebuilding took place in 1804 and the superimposed buildings 'have become pathetic travesties of the original design' (W. Ison, *The Georgian Buildings of Bath* (1948), p. 67).

119 NO. 7 QUEEN STREET, Edinburgh (patron: Lord Chief Baron Orde). The first Drawing Room, 1770–1. (Photograph: G. B. Alden, *courtesy Royal College of Physicians, Edinburgh*.)

This important house for Chief Baron Orde was carried out in accordance with Adam's plans, except that in execution the rooms on the plan were reversed left to right. As a variation from the plastered ceiling the second Drawing Room has four painted roundels surrounding a central plaster motif.

120 MELLERSTAIN, Berwickshire (patron: George Baillie). The south front from the terrace, *c.* 1770. (Photograph: A. F. Kersting.)

William Adam designed the two wings of Mellerstain, building of which began in 1725. In 1770 the centre block was inserted by Robert Adam. After thoughts of Gothicizing it all he merely added battlements and hood moulds over the windows.

It was a dull solution, but all his attention was lavished on the splendid interior (col. pls. 38–41). The terraced gardens were laid out in 1909 to designs by Sir Reginald Blomfield.

Lit: Girouard.

121 MELLERSTAIN. One of four plaster panels in the Library, *c.* 1778. (Photograph: A. F. Kersting.)

This panel is a representation of one on the tomb of the Emperor Severus at Monte del Grano, copied from a 1727 book of engravings by Bartoli. The plasterer is not known. The panel is surmounted by an effective palmette and anthemia frieze. Adam's design for the ceiling of the Library is dated 5 March 1778. (*See also* col. pl. 38.)

122 MELLERSTAIN. Ceiling of the Dining (now Music) Room, 1773. (Photograph: A. F. Kersting.)

The ceiling design for this room, coloured green and purple, is dated 7 September 1773. The centre medallion is surrounded by an octagon of flowing rinceau and fan ornament, with eagles and medallions at the four corners.

MELLERSTAIN: *see also* col. pls. 38–41.

123 WEDDERBURN CASTLE, Berwickshire (patron: Patrick Home of Billy). The south front, 1770–8. (Photograph: S.N.M.R.)

The bowed projection in the centre of the south front does much to suggest the 'movement' that the brothers wrote about as a feature of their architecture. The centre is balanced by the four-storey octagonal turrets at the corners, but the basement is rusticated as thoroughly as any Palladian villa.

Lit: Rowan, 'Wedderburn Castle'.

124 STOWE, Buckinghamshire (patron: Earl Temple). The portico, 1771. (Photograph: R. & H. Chapman, Buckingham.)

Adam's design (Soane Museum, vol. 20, no. 56) shows the intended new front to the house, which also seems to have been worked on by the amateur architect Thomas Pitt, Lord Camelford. An inscription panel bears the legend: 'This front was begun by Earl Temple in the year 1771 and finished in the year [blank]'. The architectural history of Stowe is very complex, with many workers, including Pitt and the talented Giovanni Battista Borra, altering the house and other buildings in the park.

Lit: Michael Gibbon, 'Stowe, Buckinghamshire', *Architectural History*, 20 (1977), 31–44.

125 NO. 20 ST JAMES'S SQUARE, London (patron: Sir Watkin Williams-Wynn). The Eating Room, *c.* 1772–4. (Photograph: A. F. Kersting.)

The flat ceiling is set out with shallow octagonal coffering terminating at a semicircular recess. The recess is given prominence by its flanking Corinthian columns and pilasters, the capitals of which are, unusually, in the form of ram's-head volutes. This motif also appears on the dado rail, door casings, and chimneypiece.

126 NO. 20 ST JAMES'S SQUARE. The Music Room, *c.* 1773. (Photograph: A. F. Kersting.)

This room demonstrates the skill with which Adam and Joseph Rose were able to put a complex patterned ceiling into a comparatively small room. The ceiling incorporates painted roundels by Antonio Zucchi.

NO. 20 ST JAMES'S SQUARE: *see also* col. pls. 44–6.

127 DERBY HOUSE, Grosvenor Square, London. Drawing, 37·5 × 57·5cm., 1773, inscr: 'Cieling for the Great Drawing Room at Lord Stanley's in Grosvenor Square'. *Sir John Soane's Museum*, vol. 12, no. 144 (photograph: A. C. Cooper).

Derby House was one of Adam's most splendid creations for Lord Stanley, later 12th Earl of Derby. This groin-vaulted ceiling is shown in the *Works* (vol. 2, pt 1, pl. 6) – regrettably, the house was demolished in 1862.

The drawing is coloured green, lilac, pink, and yellow, with a bright-blue ground to the centre medallion.

DERBY HOUSE: *see also* col. pl. 47.

128 THE OAKS, Epsom, Surrey (patron: Lord Stanley, later 12th Earl of Derby). Fête Pavilion for Thursday 9 June 1774. Engraving from the *Works* (vol. 1, pt 4, pl. 21).

This view is of the Supper Room and part of the Ballroom erected as part of the pavilion for Lord Stanley's Fête Champêtre at his hunting seat, The Oaks.

Lit: Bolton, *Architecture*, vol. 2, pp. 72–9.

129 THE REGISTER HOUSE, Edinburgh. Drawing, 1772, inscr: 'Elevation of the South front of a Building for the Register office in Scotland'. *Sir John Soane's Museum*, vol. 30, no. 1 (photograph: S.N.M.R.).

130 THE REGISTER HOUSE, 1774–92. (Photograph: A. F. Kersting.)

The foundation stone was laid in 1774 in Robert Adam's presence, but his frequent absence thereafter led to supervision of the building by his brother John. It was hoped to complete it by 1777, but it was still incomplete at Robert's death in 1792. The Adam block was extended between 1822 and 1834 by Sir Robert Reid, without much harm being done to the original composition – Adam's best-known public work.

131 APSLEY HOUSE, London, 1775 (patron: Lord Bathurst). The view shows the original building as designed by Adam, painted on a Meissen porcelain dessert plate, dia. 23cm., part of the Saxon Service. *V. & A. Museum*, W.M. 1119–1948 (photograph: Museum).

132 THEATRE AND MARKET HALL, Bury St Edmund's, Suffolk, 1775. (Photograph: A. F. Kersting.)

Adam reconstructed an older fabric and gave to the building an Ionic feature on each face, above a rusticated ground floor.

133 NO. 20 PORTMAN SQUARE, London (patron: the Countess of Home). South front, 1775–7. (Photograph: A. F. Kersting.)

Occupying a frontage of 20m. on the north side of Portman Square, Adam's house for Lady Home is still one of the most impressive of the London town houses. The brick façade is enriched with

Coade-stone panels and roundels, but the balcony and top storey were added at a later date. The house is now occupied by the Courtauld Institute of Art in the University of London, which has carefully restored the stairhall and state rooms.

134 NO. 20 PORTMAN SQUARE. Drawing, *c.* 1775, inscr: 'Lady Home's Staircase'. *Sir John Soane's Museum*, vol. 14, no. 116 (photograph: A. C. Cooper).

This drawing was executed as designed apart from minor modifications. The combined skills of Joseph Rose junior as plasterer and Antonio Zucchi as painter were used to effect from the dome downwards.

135 NO. 20 PORTMAN SQUARE. Stairhall, first-floor level, *c.* 1777. (Photograph: A. F. Kersting.)

The lamps intended at this level (shown on the drawing: pl. 134) were replaced by Zucchi's grisaille figures in simulated niches.

136 NO. 20 PORTMAN SQUARE. The dome and skylight, *c.* 1777. (Photograph: A. F. Kersting.)

The delicate metal skylight was probably provided by William Kinsman, who was Adam's usual supplier of such fitments.

NO. 20 PORTMAN SQUARE: *see also* col. pl. 48.

137 CULZEAN CASTLE, Ayrshire (patron: 10th Earl of Cassillis). Drawing, sketch view of the south front, *c.* 1786. *Sir John Soane's Museum*, vol. 1, no. 31 (photograph: A. C. Cooper).

The hanging gardens at the left and right of this attractive view date it to *c.* 1786, about eight years after the building of the south front.

Lit: Rowan, 'After the Adelphi', 682.

138 DRAWING BY ROBERT ADAM, 23 × 31cm., pen, ink, and watercolour on paper, *c.* 1782. *V. & A. Museum*, D1894–1889 (photograph: Museum).

The castle in the drawing set high on its rocky promontory resembles the sea front of Culzean Castle (pl. 139). The watercolour also bears resemblance to two others, one in the Mellon collection at Yale, the other at the Whitworth Gallery, Manchester.

Lit: Scottish Arts Council, *Robert Adam . . . the Picturesque Drawings*, no. 37; references cited (exhibition catalogue).

139 CULZEAN CASTLE. North front, *c.* 1790, view from the shore. (Photograph: A. F. Kersting.)

This view, which shows the dramatic siting of Culzean on the west coast of Scotland, may be compared with Adam's watercolour (pl. 138).

Culzean was depicted in Anthony Trollope's *The Eustace Diamonds* as Portray Castle, home of Lizzie Eustace.

CULZEAN CASTLE: *see also* col. pls. 49–52.

140 ALNWICK, Northumberland. Drawing, elevation, and plan, s. & d. 1784, of a castellated folly. Pen, ink, and watercolour on paper, 47·5 × 63cm., inscr: 'Elevation of a Building proposed to be erected on the top of a Ridge of Rocks near Alnwick Castle'. *The Duke of Northumberland* (photograph: Newcastle University Library).

This design (there are others in the Soane Museum and at Alnwick) was, alas, not carried out. It would surely have established Adam's reputation as a designer prepared to abandon overtones of Neo-Classicism, overtones that accompany much of his other Gothic work.

141 HULNE PRIORY, Alnwick, Northumberland (patron: 1st Duke of Northumberland). Chimneypiece in the Lord's Tower, *c.* 1778. (Photograph: A. F. Kersting.)

Two miles north-east of Alnwick Castle

are the ruins of Hulne Priory, a Carmelite house. Adam Gothicized the interior. The chimneypiece shown here, in a saloon on the first floor of the fifteenth-century Lord's Tower, has a frieze bearing heraldic devices of the Percy family.

142 ALNWICK CASTLE (patron: 1st Duke of Northumberland). Drawing, elevation of the interior of the Circular Room, 1770, pen and gouache, 49 × 62·5cm. *The Duke of Northumberland* (photograph: Newcastle University Library).

The Circular Room in the Ravine Tower of Alnwick Castle survived Salvin's reconstruction (*see* No. 143), but was demolished as unsafe in the 1880s. This design is the one that was executed.

143 ALNWICK CASTLE. Drawing for a gateway, 1778, pen, ink, and wash on paper, 24 × 28cm. Inscr. (on verso): 'Design for a Gateway, Alnwick, 1778'. *The Duke of Northumberland* (photograph: Newcastle University Library).

The Gothic work at Alnwick, which Adam designed for the 1st Duke of Northumberland (pl. 85), was, for the most part, swept away in Sir Anthony Salvin's remodelling of the Castle in 1854 for the 4th Duke.

144 BRISLEE TOWER, Alnwick Park. Drawing, elevation, and plan, 1778, pen, ink, and wash on paper, 49 × 32cm. *The Duke of Northumberland* (photograph: Newcastle University Library).

This elevation shows the stone-built Gothic-folly tower (pl. 145) on an eminence in the park at Alnwick. There are three drawings for it in the Soane Museum dated 1777 (vol. 19, nos. 156–8) and five drawings, one dated 1778, at Alnwick. The drawing reproduced here is probably an office copy.

Lit: Fleming, 'Adam Gothic'.

145 BRISLEE TOWER, 1778–9. (Photograph: A. F. Kersting.)

Eneas Mackenzie in his *View of the County of Northumberland* (1825) wrote: 'the design of this tower is the most elegant imaginable, and it is finished in the highest and most splendid style of masonry' (p. 76). The mason was probably Vincent Shepherd (*c.* 1750–1812), with internal plasterwork by Joseph Rose & Company.

146 AUCHINCRUIVE, Ayrshire (patron: Richard Oswald). Garden tower, 1778. (Photograph: S.N.M.R.)

One of the eclectic designs for which Adam – as well as his eager patrons – had a weakness. Based on Theodoric's mausoleum at Ravenna, which he had drawn in 1755 (pl. 18), it also has short towers, Renaissance detailing at the eaves, and a slated conical top.

147 OXENFOORD CASTLE, Midlothian, 1780–2 (patron: Sir John Dalrymple). (Photograph: S.N.M.R.)

This is a house rebuilt around an old tower. As at Dalquharran (pl. 148) there is the use of the central bow flanked by towers. The house was added to in 1841 by the talented architect William Burn.

148 DALQUHARRAN CASTLE, Ayrshire, 1785 (patron: Thomas Kennedy of Dunure). The south front. (Photograph: S.N.M.R.)

This impressive ruin near Girvan, surviving by the strength of its masonry, has a circular saloon that gives 'movement' to the façade by pushing out as a round tower in the centre of the south front, flanked by smaller square towers with shallow arches.

149 Part of a DRAWING, 1785, Edinburgh. Inscr: 'Perspective view of the Buildings on South Bridge, Edinburgh'. *Sir John Soane's Museum*, vol. 34, no. 2 (photograph: S.N.M.R.).

If it had been carried out, Adam's scheme for a group of 'two storied porticoes' would have 'made the Bridges the most famous Neo-classical street in Europe'

(Rowan, 'After the Adelphi', 673). Two parallel streets would have run south, one across the new bridge, the other joining with Cowgate, which ran under the bridge.

150 Design for a TRIUMPHAL ARCH, *c.* 1785, 'Sacred to Science and Learning', Edinburgh. *Sir John Soane's Museum*, vol. 31, no. 32 (photograph: S.N.M.R.).

The façade bears, in addition to the inscription in English noted above, Latin quotations and medallions dedicated to 'Geometry' and 'Architecture'. It was designed as a temporary structure on strictly Classical lines.

151 THE UNIVERSITY, Edinburgh. The main entrance, 1789–91. (Photograph: A. F. Kersting.)

The foundation stone was laid in Robert Adam's presence in 1789, but the work, as at the Register House (pl. 130), went very slowly. Adam wanted, as he wrote, to leave 'behind me a monument of my talents, such as they are', but he was near thwarted by hostility and committee dithering; he died in 1792, before the building's completion. Building was not resumed until 1815: alas, in the heavy style of Sir Robert Reid. There is further, more sympathetic, work by W. H. Playfair (1818–*c.* 1830), but the dome by Sir Rowand Anderson (1887) does little for the noble façade below it.

152 PITFOUR CASTLE, Perthshire, *c.* 1790 (patron: John Richardson). (Photograph: S.N.M.R.)

At this commission Adam tinkered away at a medieval repertory suitable for a castle. The D-shaped saloon at Pitfour is responsible for the bow front, which is given added character by the blind arches. The flanking circular turrets also have narrow arches with lancet-type windows.

153 NEWLISTON, West Lothian, 1790–2 (patron: Thomas Hog). The east front. (Photograph: John Dewar, Edinburgh.)

Late in Adam's career, Newliston was built more or less to the drawing (Soane Museum, vol. 32, no. 67), with coupled Corinthian half-columns supporting a pediment. The two wings were added in 1845 by David Bryce.

154 FITZROY SQUARE, London, 1790–1800. The east side. (Photograph: A. F. Kersting.)

It is natural to compare the Fitzroy Square scheme with that in Charlotte Square, Edinburgh (pl. 155). The London block is longer and an attic storey has been added. The repeated Venetian openings draw attention to a centrepiece with Ionic columns, and the detailing is all carried out in substantial Portland stone, with Liardet cement swags on the entablature.

155 CHARLOTTE SQUARE, Edinburgh, 1791. The central portion of the north side. (Photograph: A. F. Kersting.)

The Square was intended to be the main feature of the extension of the New Town westwards in 1791 and was to balance St Andrew's Square to the east. Adam's death and the outbreak of the French Revolution prevented all but the north side from being started, and it was 1807 before the Square was finished, as part of a compromise scheme by the City, which proved very expensive to carry out.

The north side retains the original railings and lamp standards, and survives as the most complete elevation of Adam's street architecture.

156 THE TRADES HALL, Glassford Street, Glasgow, 1791–9. (Photograph: David Wrightson.)

A late building, finished after Adam's death. Adam's designs (Soane Museum, vol. 48, nos. 23–7) are at variance with those in George Richardson's *The New Vitruvius Britannicus* (1802), where the building is called 'New Assembly Rooms' in error.

Furnishings

157 DESIGNS for a curtain cornice; bracket with a vase for candles; a candle vase; and door furniture. From the *Works* (vol. 2, pt 4, pl. 8). (Photograph: V. & A. Museum.)

Items such as these were obtained from carvers and a large group of (usually) London and Birmingham brass-founders. They are indicative of a wide decorative repertory available to Adam's patrons, and of part of his careful process of controlling the overall appearance of the objects supplied (for door furniture *see* pl. 158).

158 DOOR KNOB AND ESCUTCHEON. One of a set of five in ormolu supplied to Lord Scarsdale for the Dining Room at Kedleston, 1766. Length: 16cm. (Photograph: Raymond Fortt.)

One of the rare occasions on which Matthew Boulton was involved with the provision of door furniture. He was tardy in their supply, betokening some unfamiliarity with creating them (*see* Goodison, p. 129; also pl. 157).

159 Detail of the ORMOLU MOUNTS on the chimneypiece, *c.* 1768, in the Red Drawing Room, Syon House. (Photograph: A. F. Kersting.)

Contrary to opinion, these attractive chimney ornaments were not supplied by Matthew Boulton, whose name is too lightly invoked in respect of such ormolu mounts (Goodison, p. 23).

The Syon accounts at Alnwick (*see* Beard, *Georgian Craftsmen*, pp. 81–2) show that an obscure 'Mr Brimingham' or 'Bermingham' was responsible for the door (col. pl. 10) and shutter ornaments. His name is not a corruption for 'Birmingham' as the place of supply as the Duke's agent records Brimingham's later imprisonment. We may assume he also supplied the chimney mounts.

160 Detail of the conjoined RAMS' HEADS, carved and gilt, on one of the two side tables, Red Drawing Room, *c.* 1765, Syon House. (Photograph: A. F. Kersting.)

No drawing by Robert Adam survives but the tables and pier-glasses are illustrated in the *Works* (vol. 3, pl. 11), wrongly inscribed as for the Earl of Bute. The Roman mosaic tops in a reeded brass moulding are said to have been 'found in the Baths of Titus' and obtained at a cost of £300.

161 DRAWING by Robert Adam, 1773, inscr: 'Commode for His Grace the Duke of Bolton: Adelphi 16th January 1773'. *Sir John Soane's Museum*, vol. 17, no. 18 (photograph: A. C. Cooper).

This design was followed, with some modifications, for a pair of commodes at Osterley (Drawing Room). The drawing also shows a design (not illustrated here) for a semi-circular top. The Duke's commode was intended for Bolton House in Russell Square, London.

162 DRAWING by Robert Adam, inscr: 'Harpsichord for the Empress of Russia: Adelphi 1774'. *Sir John Soane's Museum*, vol. 25, no. 9 (photograph: A. C. Cooper).

The design was published in the *Works* (vol. 1, pt 5, pl. 8) as a plan and elevation, rather than the careful perspective of this drawing. The harpsichord is depicted as a splendidly symmetrical instrument, but we may suspect that such symmetry would not have helped the tonal quality.

163 CABINET, 188 × 177 × 40cm., made by Ince and Mayhew, 1771–5, for the Duchess of Manchester. *V. & A. Museum*, w43–1949 (photograph: Raymond Fortt; by courtesy of Nicholas Goodison from his *Ormolu: the Work of Matthew Boulton*, Phaidon Press, 1974).

The cabinet was created to display the eleven marble intarsia panels made by Baccio Capelli at Florence in 1709. Adam provided two drawings (Soane Museum, vol. 17, no. 218; vol. 27, no. 51) but the Duchess chose a variant design, which may have been provided by Adam or Ince and Mayhew. The panels were set in veneered mahogany and Boulton and Fothergill provided the ormolu mounts (pls. 164–5).

Lit: Goodison, pp. 133–4; L. O. J. Boynton, 'Italian Craft in an English Cabinet', *Country Life*, 140 (1966), 768–9; Arts Council, *The Age of Neoclassicism*, no. 1641 (exhibition catalogue).

164 A CAPITAL in the peristyle of the temple of Aesculapius. From Robert Adam's *Ruins of the Palace of the Emperor Diocletian* (pl. 69). (Photograph: Manchester University, John Rylands Library.)

The source of the ormolu mount in pl. 165.

165 The Duchess of Manchester's cabinet: DETAIL OF THE ORMOLU MOUNT on the pilasters, one of four, *c.* 1775. (Photograph: as for No. 163.)

166 DRAWING by Robert Adam, 1774, inscr: 'Design of a Bed for the Right Honourable Lord Stanley: Adelphi 7th Sepr 1774'. *Sir John Soane's Museum*, vol. 17, no. 154 (photograph: A. C. Cooper).

One of Adam's magnificent designs for beds. How practical the arrangement of two beds under one dome would have been was not put to the test. A similar piece was made for Robert Child of Osterley (col. pl. 56; pls. 167–8).

167 THE STATE BED, 1776–7, Osterley Park. (Photograph: V. & A. Museum.)

The bed corresponds very closely to the Adam design (Soane Museum, vol. 17, no. 157) dated May 1776. The valance is worked with the Child-family crest. The dome was criticized by Horace Walpole as 'too theatric, and too like a modern head-dress'; he went on to ask what Vitruvius would have thought of 'a dome decorated by a milliner'.

168 Detail of the CARVED SPHINX on the tester of the State Bed, Osterley Park. (Photograph: V. & A. Museum.)

169 Tripod Stand, gilded beech and pine, with painted plaques, Osterley Park. One of a pair, *c.* 1776. Ht 127cm. (Photograph: V. & A. Museum.)

The Soane Museum design (vol. 17, no. 62) is dated 13 November 1776, and shows a popular form deriving from a Classical incense burner.

170–1 Chair, one of a set of eight, made by John Cobb, 1764, for Croome Court. *Trustees of the Croome Estate* (photographs: Geoffrey Beard).

The detail shows the anthemion back splat and top rail, which were carved for Cobb by Sefferin Alken, one of a family of carvers employed by Adam at Sharde-loes, Croome, and elsewhere. Cobb's early adoption of the Neo-Classical style did much to further his reputation and gain him a considerable fortune.

Lit: Croome Archives, John Cobb, July 1764: 'For 8 Mahogany Arm'd Chairs the Seats Stuff'd & Coverd with blue Morroco Leather and finished with burnishd nails and Carving all the Arms and 2 front feet, all the rest carved by Mr. Alkin £30'.

172 Candelabrum, one of a set of four, by John Carter, London, 1774. *Lloyd's of London* (photograph: Worshipful Company of Goldsmiths).

Carter closely followed an Adam design (Soane Museum, vol. 25, no. 126), dated 9 March 1773, for candelabra intended for Sir Watkin Williams-Wynn at 20 St James's Square (Adam designed many pieces of silver and miscellanea for the house: from ink stands to watch cases and birdcages).

Lit: Rowe, *Adam Silver*, pls. 12–13.

Furnishings: *see also* col. pls. 53–60.

Funerary Monuments

173 Monument to the Hon. Lt-Col. Roger Townshend, *c.* 1761, Westminster Abbey. (Photograph: Helmut Gernsheim, for the Warburg Institute.)

Townshend was killed on 25 July 1759 by a cannon ball whilst reconnoitring the French lines at Triconderagoe in North America. His mother asked Adam to design the monument, which was sculpted by Thomas Carter and John Eckstein. Flaxman said that the relief, with its fine Neo-Classical scrolling and dramatic figures – for which Eckstein was responsible – was one of the best pieces of sculpture in the Abbey.

174 Drawing by Robert Adam, s. & d. 1775, inscr: 'Design of a Monument for the late Robert Wood Esq.: Adelphi 29th July 1775'. *Sir John Soane's Museum*, vol. 19, no. 57 (photograph: A. C. Cooper).

In 1750 Wood, with James Dawkins, John Bouverie, and G. B. Borra, set out to survey the Roman ruins at Palmyra (and four years later at Baalbek). The appearance of his two books about the sites in 1753 and 1757 enhanced not only his reputation but also that of the Society of Dilettanti, which had sponsored him. Adam thought highly of him, describing him as one 'whose character is one of the most perfect among the Human Race'. Wood died in 1771. Adam's design for his monument was not executed.

175 Drawing by Robert Adam, monument to Major John André, 1780. *Sir John Soane's Museum*, vol. 19, no. 29 (photograph: A. C. Cooper).

176 Detail of Monument to Major John André, 1780, Westminster Abbey, Nave, south aisle. (Photograph: Helmut Gernsheim for the Warburg Institute.)

The panel is variant from that depicted on the Adam drawing (pl. 175), but both versions show General Washington receiving André's petition that he should have a soldier's death – he was refused and hanged as a spy. The monument was sculpted by Peter Mathias Vangelder, who also worked to Adam's designs at Warkton (Duchess of Montagu, d. 1771; pl. 177) and Heston (Robert Child, d. 1782).

177 MONUMENT, 1775, to the memory of Mary, Duchess of Montagu (d. 1771), at Warkton church, Northamptonshire. Designed by Adam and sculpted by Peter Mathias Vangelder. (Photograph: A. F. Kersting.)

The Adam Influence

178 BOODLE'S CLUB, London. The Saloon, 1775, designed by John Crunden. (Photograph: A. F. Kersting.)

John Crunden, author of many books of designs, designed the façade for Boodle's with more than a sideways glance at Adam's Royal Society of Arts (pls. 112–13). The interiors, too – probably stuccoed by Joseph Rose or George Jackson – have the same feel, even to the variants of the 'Diocletian-headed' pilasters (pl. 165) and the inserted paintings.

179 THE MCINTIRE GARDEN HOUSE, Danvers, Massachusetts, 1793. (Photograph: R. K. Flachbart.)

In 1793 the architect Samuel McIntire designed and built this small Adamesque summer house for Elias Haskett Derby's farm in Danvers. The house is two and a half storeys high. It was moved to its present site in 1901 and is now ad-ministered as a registered National Historic Landmark by the Danvers Historical Society.

180 BOSCOBEL, Montrose, New York, 1804–7. (Photograph: Boscobel Restoration Inc.)

This house was built for States Morris Dyckman (1755–1806). He had spent ten years, 1779–88, in England and presumably seen much of Adam's Neo-Classical work. The house is unusual for its unique interpretation of English prototypes of a slightly earlier period. In 1955 the house was carefully moved to a new position twelve miles from the original site; it has undergone careful restoration.

181 WILLOW BROOK, Baltimore, Maryland. Ceiling of the Oval Room, *c.* 1800, re-erected 1966 at the Baltimore Museum of Art. (Photograph: Museum.)

At the end of the eighteenth century Baltimore was a centre for itinerant plasterers, many of them Irish, who worked on houses in the eastern seaboard states. Close similarities between two houses by William Thornton (Woodlawn and The Octagon) and Willow Brook suggest that Thornton also designed the Baltimore house.

The use of an oval room, such as that at Willow Brook, did not become a widespread practice in American architecture until the first part of the nineteenth century.

COLOUR PLATES

1 BINDING of a presentation copy of Robert Adam's *Ruins of the Palace of the Emperor Diocletian, at Spalatro, in Dalmatia*, folio, 1764. Red morocco, gold tooled. *The British Library*, 137 h.10 (photograph: Museum).

This copy was presented to George III by the author, and bears the Royal Arms. It is one of six in red morocco presented to various members of the royal family; a few more were bound in green for presentation to favoured Knights of the Order of the Thistle.

Lit: Nixon, 184.

The Buildings

2 CROOME COURT, Worcestershire (patron: George William, 6th Earl of Coventry). Detail of the north-west corner of the Tapestry Room, 1760–9. *Metropolitan Museum of Art, New York* (photograph: Museum).

When this room was re-erected in New York it benefited from a meticulous research programme, which concluded with full publication of all relevant details. Briefly, Lord Coventry visited Paris in 1763 and ordered a set of tapestries of thirteen pieces from the Gobelins Manufactory – similar sets at Osterley and Newby are illustrated here (col. pls. 6, 30). The Croome set was finally installed by Ince and Mayhew's men in June 1771. The various elements of the room were acquired by the Samuel H. Kress Foundation over twelve years, 1947–59, and re-erected as the Foundation's gift at the Metropolitan Museum in 1959.

Lit: *see* Bibliography: articles by Eileen Harris, and James Parker with Edith Standen.

CROOME COURT: *see also* pls. 38–41.

3 KEDLESTON, Derbyshire (patron: Sir Nathaniel Curzon, Bt, created Lord Scarsdale April 1761). The Saloon, 1761–2. (Photograph: A. F. Kersting.)

This room, with its coffered dome and niches, is the most Roman of Adam's interiors. The ruin paintings are by William Hamilton and the grisaille panels by Biagio Rebecca; both paintings and panels are indicated on the working drawing (Soane Museum, vol. 40, no. 3). The room was modified against the drawing, one particular substitution being the gilded and stucco wall sconces (Stillman, *Decorative Work*, pl. 164). The door leads to the Hall (pl. 46).

KEDLESTON: *see also* pls. 43–7.

4 OSTERLEY PARK, Middlesex (patron: Robert Child). The Drawing Room, *c.* 1773. (Photograph: A. F. Kersting.)

With its ceiling adapted from one at Palmyra published by Robert Wood (1753), its Moorfield's carpet (pls. 66–7), and pea-green silk damask walls, the room earned Walpole's high praise in 1773 as one 'worthy of Eve before the Fall'. The precision of the Neo-Classical ornament on the doorcases is repeated in a similar style on the chimneypiece (pl. 64).

5 OSTERLEY PARK. The Eating Room, *c.* 1767. (Photograph: A. F. Kersting.)

This room has an earlier ceiling than most of the Osterley rooms, which suggests that it may have been created when William Chambers was working at the house in the late 1750s. However, it bears close resemblance to one by Adam at Shardeloes, although there is no Soane

Museum design for it. The painted furniture by John Linnell, Zucchi's inset paintings of ruins, the arabesque stucco panels, and the lyre-back chairs combine to make an impressive Neo-Classical display.

6 OSTERLEY PARK. The Tapestry Room, *c*. 1773. (Photograph: A. F. Kersting.)

Walpole visited Osterley again in 1778, five years after his first visit (No. 4 above). He described this room as 'the most superb and beautiful that can be imagined', but at the same time he blamed Adam for 'sticking diminutive heads in bronze, no bigger than half a crown, into the chimney-pieces hair'. The room contains another of the magnificent sets of tapestries (*see* col. pls. 2, 30) woven by Jacques Neilson at the Gobelins tapestry works in Paris. His signature and the date 1775 are woven into the panel above the fireplace. The sofa and armchairs are upholstered in tapestry woven *en suite*.

7 OSTERLEY PARK. Drawing, 1776, inscr: 'Fire Screen for Mrs Child: Adelphi, 13 Novr. 1776'. *Sir John Soane's Museum*, vol. 17, no. 141 (photograph: A. C. Cooper).

A variant design for the embroidery, which was finally done and set into a tripod pole screen, *c*. 1777, still at Osterley (Eileen Harris, *Furniture*, pl. 144).

8 OSTERLEY PARK. The Etruscan Dressing Room, *c*. 1775–6. (Photograph: A. F. Kersting.)

This room, with decoration based on the study of Classical vases and engravings by Piranesi (pls. 72–3), survives as the most complete example of this unusual style. The room was intended as a dressing-room to the State Bedroom. The painter of the ceiling decoration – except for the central roundel – was P. M. Borgnis; the roundel is by Antonio Zucchi.

OSTERLEY PARK: *see also* pls. 56–78.

9 SYON HOUSE, Middlesex (patron: 1st

Duke of Northumberland). The Drawing Room, 1762–4.(Photograph: A.F.Kersting.)

Adam gave a great deal of attention to this richly decorated room with its unusual painted cove. It is a complex amalgam of Cipriani's painted roundels (col. pl. 11), red damask walls, ormolu decoration on door (col. pl. 10) and chimneypiece (pl. 159), and Thomas Moore's superbly coloured carpet, signed 1769.

10 SYON HOUSE. The Drawing Room, door to the Long Gallery, *c*. 1766–7. (Photograph: A. F. Kersting.)

The Syon accounts at Alnwick Castle (Beard, *Georgian Craftsmen*, p. 81) show that the ormolu decoration on the door architrave was the work of Diederich Nicolaus Anderson (Goodison, pls. 65–72). That on the door was by the mysterious 'Mr. Brimingham', who perhaps also decorated the chimneypiece (pl. 159).

11 SYON HOUSE. Detail of the Drawing Room ceiling, 1764–5. (Photograph: A. F. Kersting.)

The painter Giovanni Battista Cipriani agreed to paint the roundels, 'in the best manner', at two guineas each. He visited the house in 1765 to supervise their insertion – they are painted on paper.

12 SYON HOUSE. The Long Gallery, *c*. 1763–8. (Photograph: A. F. Kersting.)

Adam had thoughts about the decoration of this noble room as early as 1761 (Soane Museum, vol. 11, no. 22): the problem was its Jacobean length (42m.) contrasted to its meagre width and height (both measurements: 4·3m.). The solution was partly linear, with the introduction of sixty-two painted pilasters executed by Pergolesi in 1768. The gilder (1765) was Thomas Davis and the plastering was done by Joseph Rose & Company.

13 SYON HOUSE. Detail of the south-west corner, Long Gallery, *c*. 1763–8. (Photograph: A. F. Kersting.)

The Duke of Northumberland was assiduous in his attentions to what Adam was doing at Syon. He wrote on 4 November 1763 to 'very much approve' of the twisted flutings under the bookcase seen in this view. The three painted roundels (left to right) are of Charles, Duke of Somerset; Elizabeth, wife of Adam's patron, the 1st Duke; and Algernon, 7th Duke of Somerset and Earl of Northumberland. For a detail of the ceiling *see* pl. 82.

14 SYON HOUSE. Detail of panel with 'antique' stucco medallion, Long Gallery, *c.* 1763–8. (Photograph: A. F. Kersting.)

While both Adam and his stuccoist Joseph Rose junior paid attention to the Imperial-period and High Renaissance stuccoes in Rome, medallions such as this were usually based on engraved sources. Books by Bellori (Rome, 1693) the Abbé Montfaucon (English translation of 1722) and le Comte de Caylus (Paris, 1752) provided most of the subject material for copying or adaptation.

15 SYON HOUSE. The Ante-Room, *c.* 1761–5. (Photograph: A. F. Kersting.)

The visitor to Syon moves through the Entrance Hall (pl. 83), ascends steps, and enters this richly coloured room. Joseph Rose excelled with the gilded stuccoes in the Antique style, but a true touch of antiquity was provided by the columns, found in Italy, and shipped to England in 1765 (Beard, *Georgian Craftsmen*, p. 82). The two great trophy panels (one of which can be seen to the right of the door) are based on the Trophies of Marius and of Octavianus Augustus, as engraved by G. B. Piranesi in his *Trofei Di Ottaviano Augusto* (1753).

SYON HOUSE: *see also* pls. 79–87.

16 LANSDOWNE HOUSE, London (patron: 2nd Earl of Shelburne, later 1st Marquess of Lansdowne). The first Drawing Room,

1767–73. Room re-erected, 1931, *Philadelphia Museum of Art*, gift in memory of George Horace Lorimer by Graeme Lorimer and Sara Moss Lorimer (photograph: Museum).

The family moved into the incomplete house in 1768. The fine painted ceiling by Giovanni Battista Cipriani – charged for between 1771 and 1773 – differs from the Adam drawing (Soane Museum, vol. 11, no. 83). The grotesque decoration between the inset paintings and on the pilasters was provided by Zucchi at a cost of £112. The room was dismantled in 1930 and re-erected at the Philadelphia Museum in 1931. The dining room from the house was re-erected with amendments in the Metropolitan Museum of Art, New York, in 1932.

Lit: Stillman, *Decorative Work*, p. 101; pls. 30–1, 134–5.

17 AUDLEY END, Essex (patron: Sir John Griffin Griffin). The Great Drawing Room, *c.* 1762–5. (Photograph: Department of the Environment, Crown Copyright Reserved.)

Sir John Griffin Whitwell inherited in 1762 on condition that he changed his name to Sir John Griffin Griffin. This done, he set about completing, with Adam's help, work begun by his aunt, Lady Portsmouth. The ceiling is of a complexity comparable with that of the ceiling in the Long Gallery at Syon (pl. 82); the chimneypiece is the only Adam one in the house to survive in its original position. The furniture was also designed by the architect (Eileen Harris, *Furniture*, p. 48), but as late as 1771.

18–19 HAREWOOD HOUSE, Yorkshire (patron: Edwin Lascelles, 1st Earl of Harewood). Two details of the Long Gallery ceiling, *c.* 1768–9. (Photographs: A. F. Kersting.)

'This was the last room in the house to be completed and from its inception has been more subject to alteration than any other' (Mauchline, p. 84). The first designs for the ceiling are both dated 1765, but three years later Lascelles settled on the present design – a spirited assembly of various shapes, created with dexterity by Joseph Rose & Company; the painted insets are by Biagio Rebecca.

Rose's receipt for the final instalment of the £335 he charged for the Gallery (his overall bill for the Harewood work was £2,829 17s.) is dated 7 August 1770. The room was 'finished' by the wood pelmets, carved with great skill by Thomas Chippendale to represent taffeta hangings (col. pl. 18).

Lit: Mauchline, pp. 84–7; Beard, *Plasterwork*, pp. 240–1.

20 HAREWOOD HOUSE. The Music Room, *c.* 1765–71. (Photograph: A. F. Kersting.)

This room is another excellent example of the close relationship that could be achieved between ceiling and carpet design; *see also* Mrs Montagu's house (col. pls. 25–6) and Saltram (col. pl. 35). The drawings for the room date between 1765 and 1770 and one of the large ruin paintings by Zucchi is dated 1771. The chimneypiece, incorporating the lyre motif (also woven in the carpet), was carved in 1768 by John Devall the elder as the first of many for the house. The portrait over it is Sir Joshua Reynolds's study of Mrs Hall, sister of the first Countess, portrayed as Euphrosyne, one of the Three Graces. The centre of the ceiling and the other roundels were painted, according to John Jewell's tourist's guide to house (1819), by Biagio Rebecca, although they have also been attributed to Angelica Kauffmann, who painted the ovals in the Gallery pier mirrors.

21 HAREWOOD HOUSE. Drawing, dated 1767, inscr: 'Drawing for the Gentleman's Dressing Room in the Principal Apartment in HAREWOOD HOUSE proposed to be painted in the Style of the Ancients'. *Sir John Soane's Museum*, vol. 11, no. 148 (photograph: A. C. Cooper).

This ceiling, for which there is an alternative design in the Soane Museum (vol. 11, no. 149), was executed but the room itself disappeared in the work done to the house by Sir Charles Barry, *c.* 1845–55. Joseph Rose charged £125 for the plasterwork in his 1766–70 bill at Harewood (Beard, *Plasterwork*, p. 241). This implies that the alternative stucco ceiling was provided. However, John Jewell's *The Tourist's Companion* (1819, p. 36) calls it 'richly ornamented with an antique marriage', and describes other painted decoration, including 'four paintings of boys playing by Zucchi' (*see* Stillman, *Decorative Work*, pl. 133 for the stucco design).

HAREWOOD HOUSE: *see also* pls. 93–7.

22 NOSTELL PRIORY, Yorkshire (patron: Sir Rowland Winn, Bt). The Tapestry Room, 1767. (Photograph: A. F. Kersting.)

Having completed the Library (pl. 101) Adam moved to the decoration of the Drawing Room (as the Tapestry Room was known until the nineteenth century). Zucchi painted the centre of the ceiling with a scene from the story of Cupid and Psyche and lunettes representing the Liberal Arts. His fourteen painted pilasters were removed when Charles Winn acquired the set of Brussels tapestries *c.* 1820. The chimneypiece was probably executed by John Devall.

23 NOSTELL PRIORY. The Saloon, *c.* 1768–76. (Photograph: A. F. Kersting.)

Adam's first coloured drawings for this room are dated 1768. In 1770 Sir Rowland Winn's agent wrote that 'Mr Rose has finished the frame round the sealing in the Saloon, and a great part of the work is done in the Cove'. The ceiling was painted in 1773, but Zucchi's paintings, principally of ancient ruins, were still arriving in 1776 – they were inserted over the doors and as large canvases over the chimneypiece and on the walls.

24 NOSTELL PRIORY. The Top Hall, *c.* 1773–5. (Photograph: A. F. Kersting.)

Chronologically, this room is almost at the end of Adam's work at Nostell. A detailed scheme for the walls was drawn in 1771, but it was not until September 1774 that Adam wrote: 'I am just now making out a new Section and ceiling for your Hall . . . it is now so different from anything of the kind yet executed, that I am almost persuaded you will approve of my new idea'. The stone chimneypieces were made to Adam's design by Christopher Theakstone of Doncaster. The colza-oil chandelier was supplied about 1820.

NOSTELL PRIORY: *see also* pls. 100–1.

25 DRAWING, 1766, inscr: 'Cieling of a room at Mrs Montagu's House in Hill Street'. *Sir John Soane's Museum*, vol. 11, no. 200 (photograph: A. C. Cooper).

On 11 October 1766 Adam wrote to Mrs Montagu: 'I hope this month we shall nearly finish your Room in Hill Street, The Gilders are at work, and I am doing all I can to push them on; my long absence from Town has made them more Dilatory than they otherways would have been' (Bolton, *Architecture*, vol. 2, p. 319). The square ceiling, with its chinoiserie motifs (rare in Adam's work) surrounding the centre circle, was echoed in the carpet design (col. pl. 26).

26 DRAWING, *c.* 1766, inscr: 'Carpet for Mrs Montagu'. *Sir John Soane's Museum*, vol. 17, no. 166 (photograph: A. C. Cooper).

The skill of Robert Adam in drawing the various components of a room into close stylistic relationships is rarely better expressed than in his drawings for Mrs Montagu's house. The roundels at the ceiling corners have been replaced by ovals of gay Chinese figures, and there are subtle variations in the border. The carpet was presumably moved in the mid 1770s to Mrs Montagu's new house in Portman

Square, which was, alas, destroyed by fire in 1941.

27 NEWBY HALL, Yorkshire (patron: William Weddell). The Library (originally Dining Room), *c.* 1769–70. (Photograph: A. F. Kersting.)

The room has an apse at each end divided from the centre by wooden columns with Corinthian capitals. At the far end is one of the four alabaster urns mounted on painted pedestals (drawing: Soane Museum, vol. 6, no. 56) – the other three are in the present dining room. The arabesque stucco panels and the painted insets on the walls and ceiling (col. pl. 28) seem the richer for being disposed within the smaller room of the original 1705 house.

28 NEWBY HALL. Detail of the Library ceiling, *c.* 1770. (Photograph: A. F. Kersting.)

Antonio Zucchi provided this painted oval depicting the triumph of Bacchus over Ariadne, as well as panels on the wall and overmantel, and within the Tapestry Room (col. pls. 29–30, 32). It will be recalled that in mythology Bacchus found Ariadne weeping over the desertion of Theseus. He fell in love with her and married her. (*See also* pl. 103.)

29 NEWBY HALL. Detail of the Tapestry Room ceiling, *c.* 1770. (Photograph: A. F. Kersting.)

Adam provided a design for this ceiling in 1769 (Soane Museum, vol. 8, no. 103) and it was painted by Zucchi with eleven medallions of Classical and allegorical subjects, 'including Apollo alighting from his chariot, his horses being watered by the Hours; the seasons, etc.'

30 NEWBY HALL. Detail of the Tapestry Room (originally the Drawing Room), *c.* 1770–5. (Photograph: A. F. Kersting.)

The Boucher-Neilson Gobelins tapestries (one of the five sets introduced to England by Adam's patrons) are of a different ground colour to the sets made for Croome (col. pl. 2) and Osterley (col. pl. 6). As the room is always shuttered they have stayed brilliant and completely captivate the onlooker with their *trompe l'oeil* frames, birds, and swags of flowers. The carpet was designed in 1775 (Soane Museum, vol. 17, no. 194).

31 NEWBY HALL. The Entrance Hall, *c.* 1771. (Photograph: A. F. Kersting.)

In the halls at Osterley (pl. 59) and Harewood (pl. 94) Adam incorporated stucco panels of military trophies, a pattern he continued at Newby. One of those on the west wall has the date '1771' incorporated. The room is dominated by the large canvas of sheep, goats, and cattle by Rosa da Tivoli, the mahogany-cased organ (col. pl. 58), and the black, white, and grey Sicilian-marble floor.

32 NEWBY HALL. Drawing, *c.* 1770, inscr: 'Design of a cieling for the Drawing Room at Newby'. *Cumbria County Record Office*, Pennington-Ramsden MSS. (photograph: Solway Studio, Carlisle).

This drawing shows a variation in subject to the Zucchi painted panels, but the overall disposition is as executed (col. pl. 29). The drawing has been stained by damp but still gives an accurate and colourful idea of the intended scheme.

33 NEWBY HALL. The Sculpture Gallery, 1767–72. (Photograph: A. F. Kersting.)

Weddell acquired Newby Hall about 1750 and it owes much of its present character (pls. 102–6) to him. Shortly after his return from Italy with a large collection of sculptures he commissioned Adam to add a gallery to the older house (pl. 102) to display them. The architect provided designs, some of which are in the house (pl. 104), some of which are at the Soane Museum (vol. 11, nos. 236–7; vol. 41, nos. 77–9), and arranged the room

as three chambers, the central one domed. This view shows, at the left centre, the Baberini *Venus* found in the cellars of the Barberini Palace by Gavin Hamilton, 'restored' by Pietro Pacelli, and acquired by Weddell with the help of the banker and art dealer Thomas Jenkins.

NEWBY HALL: *see also* pls. 102–6.

34 KENWOOD, Middlesex (patron: William Murray, 1st Earl of Mansfield). The Library, 1767–9. (Photograph: A. F. Kersting.)

This has been called 'Adam's finest room' (Stillman, *Decorative Work*, p. 71) and it has many obvious claims to the title. David Martin's portrait of Lord Mansfield is over the chimneypiece, which is flanked by bookcases, and the whole room is enclosed by a magnificent tunnel-vault ceiling. The room follows the 1767 drawings (Soane Museum, vol. 11, nos. 112–13; vol. 14, nos. 113–15; vol. 22, no. 234) and that in the *Works*. The plasterwork, some gilded (pl. 109), is by Joseph Rose & Company, and Zucchi provided many paintings for the room, and a ceiling centre roundel, *The Choice of Hercules*. His bill is dated in 1769.

KENWOOD: *see also* pls. 107–10.

35 SALTRAM, Devon (patron: John Parker). The Dining Room, 1768–9; remodelled 1780–1. (Photograph: A. F. Kersting.)

With the Saloon (pl. 111) and Dining Room Adam gave John Parker two distinguished rooms in his mature style. The Dining Room was originally designed (Soane Museum, vol. 11, no. 256) as a Library – Zucchi painted all the wall and ceiling paintings in 1769 (Beard, *Georgian Craftsmen*, p. 85) – but in 1785 John Parker decided to make the change. In the wall spaces left by the removal of books larger decorative paintings by Zucchi were set into carved wood frames. The suite of carved and painted furniture by Linnell (not shown) also dates from this time.

Lit: Nigel Neatby (ed.), *Saltram: The Parker Collection* (1977), pp. 38–40.

SALTRAM: *see also* pl. 111.

36 PAINTED ROUNDEL. *The Three Graces* by Antonio Zucchi, *c.* 1772. *Mr Jocelyn E. B. Stevens* (photograph: A. F. Kersting).

This roundel, representing the Three Graces dancing to the music of Eros, was set in the centre of Robert Adam's Drawing Room ceiling at No. 4 Royal Terrace, Adelphi. It was surrounded by fourteen other painted medallions by Zucchi. When the Adelphi (pl. 114) was demolished in 1936 the paintings (pl. 116) were saved, and passed through the London antique trade.

Lit: Bolton, *Architecture*, vol. 2, p. 33; 'Robert Adam's Drawing Room' (anon.).

37 NO. 6 ROYAL TERRACE, ADELPHI, London. Drawing, 1769, inscr: 'Ceiling of the front Drawing room at No. 6 Royal Terrace, Adelphi: 1769'. *Sir John Soane's Museum*, vol. 13, no. 30 (photograph: A. C. Cooper).

At the demolition of the Adelphi in 1936 the ceiling from David Garrick's house was saved. It was then presented to the V. & A. Museum by the National Art Collections Fund, and was re-erected in the Museum. The ceiling has recently undergone a careful conservation programme, which has done much to restore its original brilliance.

THE ADELPHI: *see also* pls. 112–16.

38 MELLERSTAIN, Berwickshire (patron: George Baillie). The Library, 1770–1. (Photograph: A. F. Kersting.)

This room, with its four long stucco panels (for a detail *see* pl. 121) and busts by Scheemakers and Roubiliac in the niches, may be counted as among the very finest work of Adam's mature period. The detail in the room – in chimneypiece, pel-

mets, bookcases, and frieze – adds up, as Professor Mark Girouard has noted, 'to an effect of perfection'.

Lit: Girouard.

39 MELLERSTAIN. Detail of the centre of the Library ceiling, *c.* 1770–1. (Photograph: A. F. Kersting.)

It may be assumed that painted roundels such as this in Adam's Scottish interiors were still provided by experienced painters such as Antonio Zucchi. In oil on paper or on canvas it would be a comparatively simple task to provide them to a measured drawing and fit them in position without the necessity of a visit by the artist.

40 MELLERSTAIN. Ceiling of the Corner Dressing Room, *c.* 1775. (Photograph: A. F. Kersting.)

The plasterers Adam used in Scotland are less well known than his usual London firm of Joseph Rose & Company. It would seem that Thomas Clayton junior was a favourite; in addition a number of plasterers who worked at Inveraray Castle would have been capable of ceilings such as this. The stylized vases were often variants of those in Hamilton's famous collection, published with a commentary by P. F. Hugues at Naples, 1766–7.

41 MELLERSTAIN. The Drawing Room, *c.* 1778. (Photograph: A. F. Kersting.)

The ceiling, designed in March 1778, is, with its panels of vases and attendant griffins, a pleasing symmetrical arrangement. The fine chimneypiece, *c.* 1825, is a replacement (signed J. Marshall) for the one provided by Adam. The main portraits are (left) of George Baillie's elder brother, George, and his sister Rachel, painted in 1740 when they were children by Allan Ramsay, and (over the chimneypiece) the *Principe d'Augri* by Van Dyck.

MELLERSTAIN: *see also* pls. 120–2.

42 NORTHUMBERLAND HOUSE, London

(patron: 1st Duke of Northumberland). Detail of Drawing, *c.* 1773. Inscr: 'Section of the Drawing Room Northumberland House, London'. *Sir John Soane's Museum*, vol. 39, no. 7 (photograph: A. C. Cooper).

For a description of this commission see No. 43 below.

43 NORTHUMBERLAND HOUSE. Detail of the Glass Drawing Room, *c.* 1773–5. Re-erected in the V. & A. Museum (photograph: Museum).

A few bills for this lavish room survive at Alnwick. It was altered a little from the Adam designs, possibly because of the unusual nature of the task. The green-painted glass for pilasters, frieze, and dado, with the glass walls painted red to simulate porphyry, give a brilliant effect. This is enhanced by the gilded decoration. The room was demolished in 1874, and is now at the V. & A. Museum. It has been the subject of detailed research by the curatorial staff.

Lit: W. Reider and D. Owsley, 'The Glass Drawing Room'.

44 & **46** NO. 20 ST JAMES'S SQUARE, London, 1772–4 (patron: Sir Watkin Williams-Wynn). Details of the Great Drawing Room ceiling. *The Distillers' Company* (photographs: A. F. Kersting).

Apart from Zucchi's account, the plasterer Joseph Rose junior received £2,684 for all his work at the house – one of the most important tasks of his career if it is borne in mind that his considerable Harewood commission amounted to only about £150 more.

45 NO. 20 ST JAMES'S SQUARE. Drawing, 1772, inscr: 'Ceiling of the 2nd Drawing Room at Sir Watkin Wynn's in St. James's Square; Adelphi 2nd Sepr 1772'. *Sir John Soane's Museum*, vol. 12, no. 53 (photograph: A. C. Cooper).

Zucchi's bill (National Library of Wales, Williams-Wynn MSS.) for painting at 20 St James's Square amounted to

£614 14s. (1774–6). All the subjects are listed. For the six rectangular panels he charged £25 each; for the six circles in the apses (col. pl. 46) £40 each; and for the semi-circles (col. pl. 44), with two figures and a tripod in each, £3 each.

NO. 20 ST JAMES'S SQUARE: *see also* pls. 125–6.

47 DERBY HOUSE, Grosvenor Square, London (patron: Lord Stanley, later [1776–] 12th Earl of Derby). Drawing, 1774, inscr: 'Chimney Piece for the Bow Dressing Room one pair Story at Lord Stanley's in Grosvenor Square, 1774'. *Sir John Soane's Museum*, vol. 23, no. 51 (photograph: A. C. Cooper).

The delicate carved mirror, which surmounts a chimneypiece that has coloured scagliola insets, bears a resemblance to the one Adam designed for the Glass Drawing Room (col. pl. 43) at Northumberland House (Soane Museum, vol. 22, no. 55; Stillman, *Decorative Work*, pl. 109).

DERBY HOUSE: *see also* pl. 127.

48 NO. 20 PORTMAN SQUARE, London (patron: the Countess of Home). Drawing, 1775, inscr: 'ceiling for the Drawing Room at Lady Home's in Portman Square: not executed: Adelphi 25 March 1775'. *Sir John Soane's Museum*, vol. 12, no. 165 (photograph: A. C. Cooper).

There are two other designs for this ceiling (vol. 12, nos. 166–7), all of the same date. The actual ceiling has inset painted medallions by Zucchi.

Lit: Margaret Whinney, *Home House* (1969), pp. 47–50.

NO. 20 PORTMAN SQUARE: *see also* pls. 133–6.

49 CULZEAN CASTLE, Ayrshire (patron: 10th Earl of Cassillis). Detail of the exterior, *c.* 1777–80, from the south-west. (Photograph: A. F. Kersting.)

With its four round towers and the higher central section incorporating the old sixteenth-century tower-house Culzean owes a debt (as Professor Alistair Rowan has noted) to Wedderburn (pl. 123) – 'not only in the enhanced massing and movement of the façade, but also in the hybrid idiom that combines classical string courses and an arcaded centre with cross slits on the towers and angle bartizans' (Rowan, 'After the Adelphi', 682–3). For a drawing of the south front of Culzean and a view of the house from the shore *see* pls. 137, 139.

50 CULZEAN CASTLE. The Round Drawing Room, *c.* 1790. (Photograph: A. F. Kersting.)

The disposing of doors and windows and the setting-out of a ceiling in a circular room brought out the best in Adam's craftsmen. The ceiling drawings at the Soane Museum (vol. 14, nos. 59–66) do not refer to this room, but the one at Culzean of 1790 is as executed. The carpet was also made for the room. With the oval staircase this room (which has fine sea views) was added in the second phase of building at Culzean – the anonymous author of *A Tour . . . to the Western Highlands of Scotland* (1788) wrote (p. 119): 'his Lordship, not content with the present extensive pile, intends adding a similar front to the sea, which will be a most arduous undertaking from the vast depth of the foundations necessary to be formed' (*see* pl. 139).

51 CULZEAN CASTLE. The Oval Staircase, 1787. (Photograph: A. F. Kersting.)

Adam had it in mind from the early 1760s to design an oval staircase, and he achieved the aim finally with great distinction at Culzean. He had proposed one at Great Saxham, Suffolk, for Hutchinson Mure in 1779 but his second plans for rebuilding after the fire there were not accepted. He proposed another in an unexecuted design (Soane Museum, vol.

36, no. 52) of 1789 at Cullen House, Banffshire, for the Earl of Findlater. But that at Culzean stands supreme, rising on two tiers of twelve columns each to an oval dome.

52 CULZEAN CASTLE. The Dining Room, *c.* 1780. (Photograph: A. F. Kersting.)

A particularly successful feature of the 'Adam style' was the screening of the end of a room by an entablature supported by Corinthian columns. It is used to advantage here, and in the Library at Newby (col. pl. 27).

CULZEAN CASTLE: *see also* pls. 137–9.

Furnishings

53 THE PRINCESS ROYAL'S SITTING ROOM (formerly State Bedroom), Harewood House. Detail of the recess, *c.* 1768, and Thomas Chippendale's 'Diana and Minerva' commode, 1773. (Photograph: A. F. Kersting.)

The bed was originally put in the then much deeper recess between the Ionic columns. The room, which subsequently became the Princess Royal's sitting room, contains a splendid ceiling by Joseph Rose (charged at £128), some of the best watercolours in the collection, and a superb Neo-Classical commode provided by Thomas Chippendale and itemized in his Harewood account, 12 November 1773: 'A very large rich commode . . . Doors, with Diana and Minerva and their Emblems Curiously Inlaid . . . £86'.

54 SUITE OF FURNITURE for the Dining Room, Harewood House, by Thomas Chippendale, 1769–71. (Photograph: A. F. Kersting.)

The sideboard, two pedestals with urns, and a wine cooler form one of the best-known suites of Chippendale's furniture. The researches of Mr Christopher Gilbert

('Chippendale's Harewood Commission', *Furniture History Society Journal*, 9, 1973) have established that Chippendale's men were involved with it between 1769 and 1771.

Lit: Arts Council, *The Age of Neoclassicism*, no. 1646; references cited (exhibition catalogue); Christopher Gilbert, *Thomas Chippendale* (2 vols., 1978).

55 DRAWING OF A SOFA, 1764, 19 Arlington Street, London. Inscr: 'Sopha for Sir Laurence Dundass. Baronet', s. & d. 'Robt Adam, Architect, 1764'. *Sir John Soane's Museum*, vol. 17, no. 74 (photograph: A. C. Cooper).

This is recorded in Adam's bill to Sir Laurence Dundas, 18 July 1765: 'To a Design of sopha Chairs for the Salon £5'. The sofa, with three of four chairs *en suite*, was sold at Sotheby's on 6 June 1947, as lot 154. It forms the only documented occasion so far discovered on which Adam and Chippendale collaborated as designer and cabinet-maker. Chippendale invoiced the suite to Sir Laurence in July 1765.

Lit: Anthony Coleridge, 'Sir Laurence Dundas and Chippendale', *Apollo*, 86 (1967), 199, in an issue devoted to the Dundas collections; Christopher Gilbert, *Thomas Chippendale* (2 vols., 1978).

56 DRAWING, 1776, Osterley Park. Inscr: 'Design of a Bed for Robert Child Esq: Adelphi, 16th May, 1776'. *Sir John Soane's Museum*, vol. 17, no. 157 (photograph: A. C. Cooper).

For the bed, and a detail, *see* pls. 167–8 and the accompanying notes.

57 DRAWING, 1781, Cumberland House, Pall Mall, London. Inscr: 'Design for organ case for His Royal Highness the Duke of Cumberland: Adelphi 2 May 1781'. *Sir John Soane's Museum*, vol. 25, no. 18 (photograph: A. C. Cooper).

The refinement of this organ case over the heavier one at Newby (col. pl. 58) of some ten years earlier is marked. It has a very slight resemblance in colour and decoration to that designed by James Wyatt in 1790 for Heaton Hall, Manchester (Bicentenary Exhibition catalogue, Manchester City Art Gallery [1972], no. 58 *repr.* in colour). That example was painted by Biagio Rebecca. As decoration in the Etruscan style is indicated on this drawing Rebecca may have been involved in this splendid example, which has not, alas, survived.

58 The ORGAN in the Entrance Hall, Newby Hall, *c.* 1771. (Photograph: A. F. Kersting.)

Adam provided organs for a number of patrons, including Lord Scarsdale (1770) and the Duke of Cumberland (col. pl. 57). We may perhaps assume that this example (as at Kedleston) was gilded by Mr Gamble, and that its mahogany case of architectural form was enhanced with carving by James Gravenor.

59 CANDLESTICK. One of a pair, by John Carter, London, 1767. Ht 34·6cm. *Leeds City Art Galleries*, 9/63 (photograph: Gilchrist of Leeds).

The pair of candlesticks in the Leeds collection is part of a larger set. It follows designs by James (and possibly Robert) Adam (Soane Museum, vol. 25, no. 97).

Lit: Rowe, *Adam Silver*, pls. 11 a & b.

60 ANGLESEY CUP. This cup, made in 1764 to an Adam design, was added to the Anglesey Abbey collection by the 1st Lord Fairhaven. *The National Trust* (photograph: John Bethell).

Lit: Rowe, *Adam Silver*, pls. 8–9; Robert Rowe, 'English Silver', *Treasures of the National Trust*, ed. R. Fedden (1976), pl. 154; Arts Council, *The Age of Neoclassicism*, no. 1746 (exhibition catalogue).

THE PLATES

1   Robert Adam. Detail of portrait by
George Willison, *c.* 1773   ▷

△ 2   William Adam, Robert's father, by William Aikman, *c.* 1727

△ 3   Mary Adam, Robert's mother, by Allan Ramsay, *c.* 1754

△ 4   John Adam, Robert's elder brother, attrib. to Francis Cotes, *c.* 1750

△ 5   Robert Adam. Portrait by George Willison, *c.* 1773

△ 6 James Adam, Robert's younger brother, by Allan Ramsay, c. 1754

7 Robert Adam. Miniature by Laurent Pecheux, c. 1755 ▷

△ 8 Robert Adam. Tassie medallion, *c.* 1792

△ 9 Robert Adam. Tassie medallion, *c.* 1793

▽ 10 Detail of Piranesi's dedicatory plate, 1756, showing his head and that of Adam

△ 12 Drawing of a Gothic church, by Robert Adam, 1753

△ 11 Drawing of a Gothic tower, by Robert Adam, 1753

▽ 13 Drawing of a Gothic folly, by Robert Adam, 1749

△ 14 Drawing of a temple, by Robert Adam, 1753

△ 15 Drawing of a funerary monument, by Robert Adam, *c.* 1756

▽ 16 Detail of a drawing of a palace, by Robert Adam, *c.* 1756

△ 17   Drawing by C.-L. Clérisseau, Arch
of Augustus, Rimini, 1755

△ 18   Drawing by Robert Adam, Mausoleum of Theodoric, Ravenna, 1755

△ 19 Drawing by Robert Adam, Hadrian's Villa, nr Tivoli, 1756

20 Drawing by Robert Adam of fallen masonry, c. 1756 ▷

◁ 21 Hopetoun House. Centre of E. front, 1721–

△ 22 Hopetoun House. E. front, 1721–54

▽ 23 Hopetoun House. N. pavilion, 1752–4

△ 24

△ 25

24–5 Hopetoun House. Details of ceiling
plasterwork, Red Drawing Room, *c.* 1754

26 Hopetoun House. Red Drawing
Room, *c.* 1754   ▷

△ 27   Hopetoun House. Ceiling plaster-work, Yellow Drawing Room, *c.* 1752

▽ 28   Hopetoun House. Chimneypiece, Red Drawing Room

△ 29 Fort George. Detail of fortifications, *c.* 1753

▽ 30 Fort George. The Ravelin Gate, *c.*
1753

△ 31 Pollok House. Erected by John and
Robert Adam, 1752–

▽ 32 Dumfries House. By John and
Robert Adam, 1754–9

△ 33   Hatchlands. W. front, *c.* 1758   ▽ 34   Hatchlands. Detail of Library ceiling, *c.* 1759

△ 35 Hatchlands. Detail of Dining
Room ceiling, *c.* 1759

36

36 Shardeloes. E. front, 1759–61 △ 37 Shardeloes. Detail of Hall ceiling, 1761–3

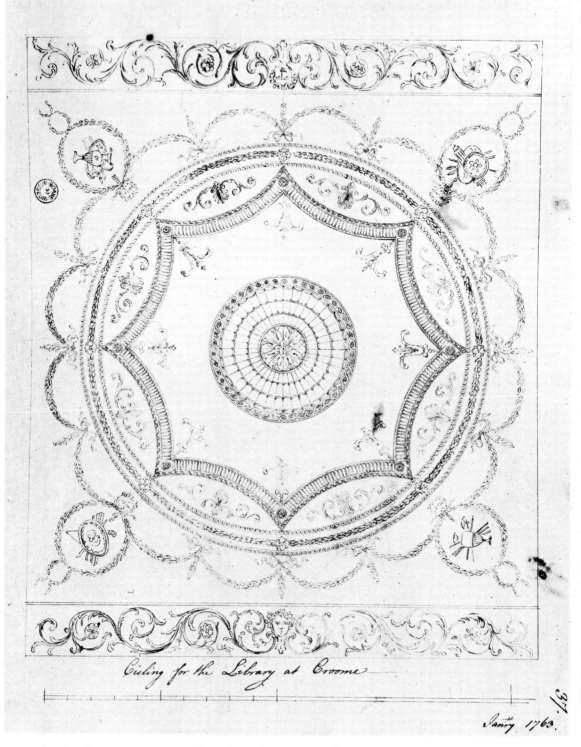

Ceiling for the Library at Croome

Jan.ry 1763

△ 38 Croome Court. Drawing by
Robert Adam of Tapestry Room ceiling,
1763

△ 39 Croome Court. Tapestry Room
ceiling, 1763

△ 40 Croome Court. Gallery, 1761–6 ▽ 41 Croome Court. Garden Temple, *c.* 1765

△ 42

△ 43

42 Admiralty Screen, Whitehall, 1760–1,
engraving 1775

43 Kedleston. Painting of N. front and
garden buildings, c. 1765

△ 44   Kedleston. S. front, 1760–5

▽ 45   Kedleston. Drawing by Robert Adam for Library, 1768

△ 46   Kedleston. Hall: chimneypiece on W. wall, *c.* 1765

△ 47 Kedleston. Dining Room, 1760–

48 ▷

48 Shambles and Butter Market, High
Wycombe, Bucks., 1761

▽ 49 Compton Verney. Adam wings
and portico, c. 1765

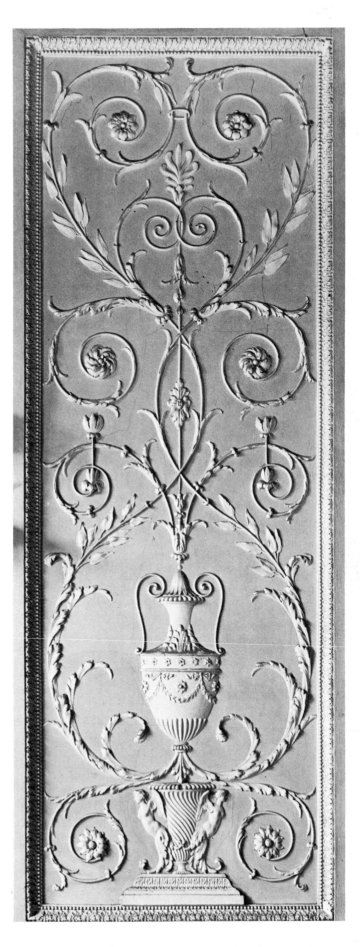

△ 52 Bowood. Ceiling of 'King's Room', *c.* 1763

▽ 53 Bowood. Detail of Entrance Hall balcony, *c.* 1768

△ 54 Bowood. 'Diocletian' wing from   ▽ 55 Bowood. Mausoleum, 1761–3
roof of the 'Big House', 1769–70

△ 56   Osterley Park. Portico, *c.* 1762   ▽ 57   Osterley Park. View from inner courtyard through portico.

△ 58   Osterley Park. Soffit of portico

△ 59 Osterley Park. Entrance Hall, 1767–8

▽ 60 Osterley Park. Drawing by Robert Adam, Entrance Hall ceiling, 1767

△ 61 Osterley Park. Plaster trophy panel, Entrance Hall, 1767

▽ 62 Osterley Park. Glass and ormolu lantern, *c.* 1770

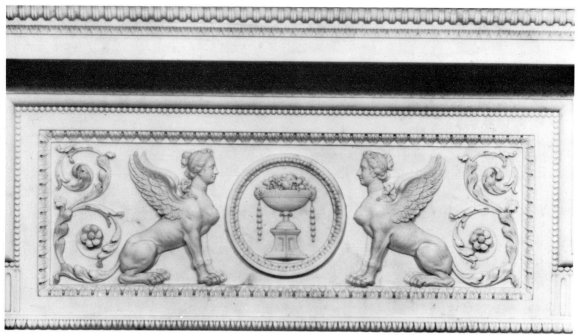

△ 64

◁ 63 Osterley Park. Staircase, 1768

64 Osterley Park. Centre panel of Drawing Room chimneypiece, c. 1772

65 Osterley Park. Detail of door architrave, Drawing Room, c. 1772 ▷

△ 66 Osterley Park. Design for Drawing Room carpet, *c.* 1773

▽ 67 Osterley Park. Detail, Drawing Room carpet, *c.* 1773

△ 68 Osterley Park. Library, 1766–73   ▽ 69 Osterley Park. Chimneypiece detail, Etruscan Dressing Room, *c.* 1777

△ 70   Osterley Park. Door in Etruscan   71   Osterley Park. Detail of door in
Dressing Room, *c.* 1776   pl. 70   ▷

△ 72   G. B. Piranesi. Detail of design for
a chimneypiece and wall, 1769

△ 73 Osterley Park. Preliminary design,
Etruscan Dressing Room, *c.* 1775

Chimney board for the Etruscan Dressing room at Osterly —

Adelphi

△ 74 Osterley Park. Drawing of chimneyboard, 1777

△ 75 Osterley Park. Chimneyboard,
State Bedroom, 1778

△▽ 76–7 Osterley Park. Details of State
Bedroom chimneypiece, *c.* 1777

△ 78   Osterley Park. Ceiling of Etruscan
Grotto, 1779

△ 79 Syon House. W. front (cased in
Bath stone *c.* 1825)

▽ 80 Syon House. Detail of ceiling in
Dining Room apse, *c.* 1764

△ 81   Syon House. Detail of Drawing Room ceiling, *c.* 1766

▽ 82   Syon House. Detail of Long Gallery ceiling, *c.* 1766

◁ 83 Syon House. Entrance Hall, *c.*   △ 84 Syon House. Dining Room, *c.*
1761–   1761–9

△ 85   Syon House. Detail of Long Gallery, 1766–8, showing portrait of 1st Duke
of Northumberland

86   Syon House. Perspective view of
bridge, 1768

87   Syon House. Entrance gateway and
screen, *c.* 1773   ▷

△ 88 Transparency in honour of George III's birthday, 1762

90 Mersham Le Hatch. Detail of Drawing Room ceiling, 1766 ▷

▽ 89 Mersham Le Hatch. S. front, 1762–5

△ 91 Croome D'Abitot. Detail of Gothic pulpit tester, *c.* 1763

△ 92 Ugbrooke Park. S. and W. fronts, 1764–8

2. Design of a Chimney Piece for the Gallery at Harewood

△ 93 Harewood House. Drawing for Gallery chimneypiece, 1771

94 Harewood House. Entrance Hall, *c.* 1765–7

▷

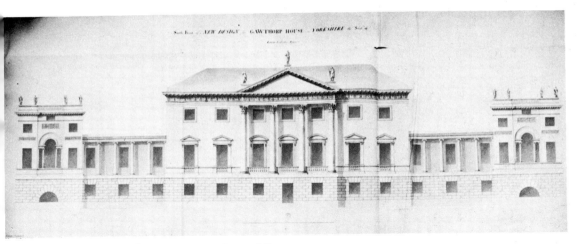

△ 96 Harewood House. Drawing of S.
front, *c.* 1761

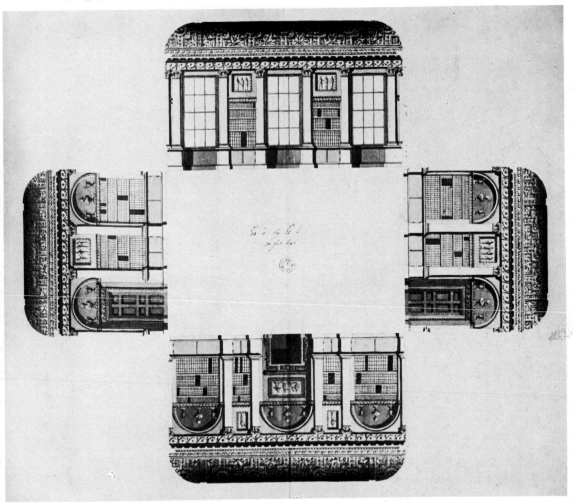

△ 97 Harewood House. Drawing of
Library, 1765

◁ 95 Harewood House. Library chimneypiece, *c.* 1769

△ 98   Kimbolton Castle. Gate House, *c.*
1765

▽ 99   Strawberry Hill. Round Drawing
Room chimneypiece, *c.* 1766

△ 100 Nostell Priory. Drawing of
Saloon ceiling, *c.* 1767

▽ 101 Nostell Priory. Library, 1766–7

◁ 102 Newby Hall. S. front (*c.* 1705)
with Adam wing, *c.* 1767–76

▽ 104

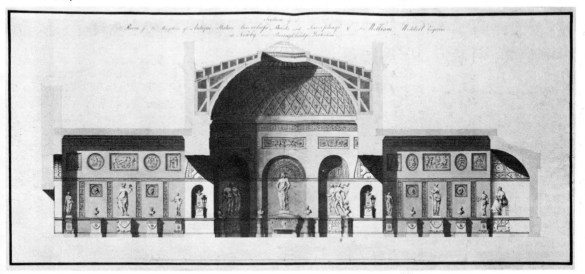

△ 105

◁ 103 Newby Hall. Detail of Library
chimneypiece, *c.* 1770

104 Newby Hall. Drawing, section of
Sculpture Gallery, *c.* 1767

105 Newby Hall. Drawing of Library
ceiling, 1767

△ 106 Newby Hall. Staircase Hall, *c.*
1768

▽ 107 Kenwood. Portico on N. front, *c.*
1769–70

△ 108　Joseph Rose junior, plasterer, self-portrait in crayons, *c.* 1790

△ 109　Kenwood. Gilded plasterwork in Library, 1769

△ 110　Kenwood. Engraving of Library ceiling, 1767, published 1773

ARTS AND COMMERCE PROMOTED.

◁ 111   Saltram. Saloon, 1768–9   △ 112   The Adelphi. Elevation of Royal
Society of Arts, engraved 1775

△ 113   Adelphi. Royal Society of Arts, 1772–4

△ 114   Adelphi. Royal Terrace

◁ 115   Adelphi. The arches, *c.* 1768

116   Adelphi. Ceiling in No. 4 Royal
Terrace   ▷

△ 117 Gunton church, 1769

▽ 118 Pulteney Bridge. Aquatint by Thomas Malton, 1788

△ 119   No. 7 Queen Street, Edinburgh. First Drawing Room, 1770–1

△ 120   Mellerstain. S. front from terrace,   ▽ 121   Mellerstain. Plaster panel, Library,
c. 1770   *c.* 1778

△ 122   Mellerstain.   Ceiling of Dining
(now Music) Room, 1773

△ 123   Wedderburn. S. front, 1770–8   ▽ 124   Stowe. Portico, 1771

△ 125 No. 20 St James's Square, London.
Eating Room, *c.* 1772–4

△ 126 No. 20 St James's Square, London.
Music Room, *c.* 1773

△ 127 Derby House. Design for ceiling in Great Drawing Room, 1773 ▽ 128 The Oaks, Epsom. Fête Pavilion, 1774

THE BUILDINGS

▽ 129   Register House, Edinburgh. Elevation of S. front, 1772

△ 130   Register House, Edinburgh. S. front, 1774–92

131 Apsley House, London, 1775. Painted
on a Meissen plate ▽

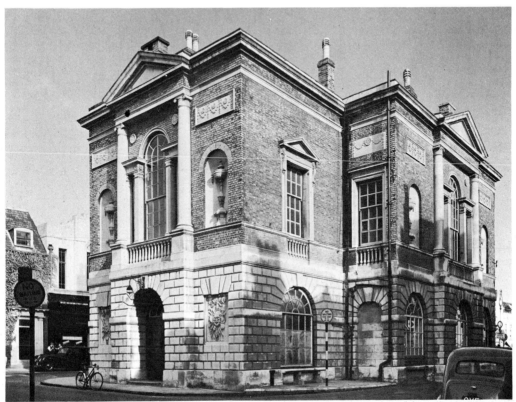

△ 132 Theatre and Market Hall, Bury St
Edmund's, 1775

△ 133   No. 20 Portman Square, London.
S. front, 1775–7

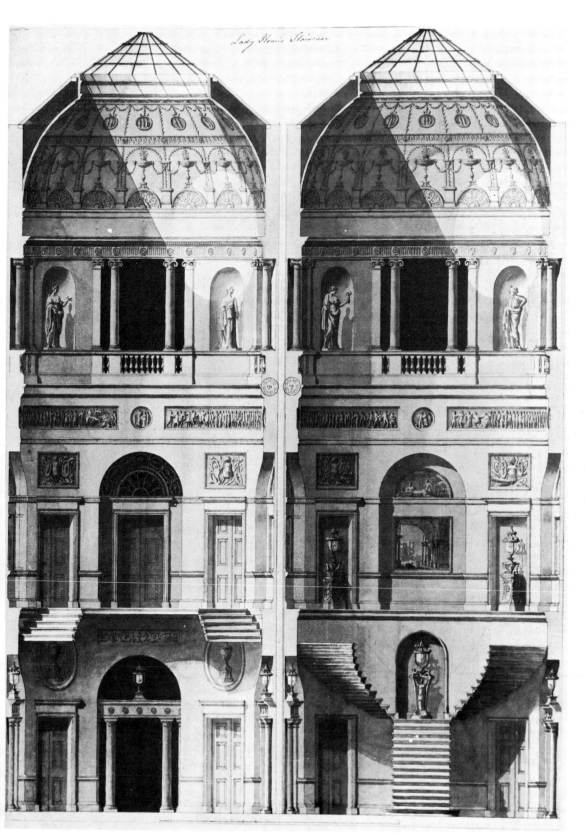

△ 134   No. 20 Portman Square, London.
Drawing of staircase, c. 1775

△ 135 No. 20 Portman Square, London.
Stairhall, first floor, c. 1777

△ 136   No. 20 Portman Square, London.
Dome and skylight, *c.* 1777

△ 137 Culzean Castle. Drawing of S. front, *c.* 1786

▽ 138 Drawing of castle by Robert Adam, *c.* 1782

△ 139 Culzean Castle. N. front, *c.* 1790, from the shore

▽ 140 Alnwick. Drawing of a castellated folly, 1784

△ 141 Hulne Priory, Alnwick. Chimneypiece, Lord's Tower, *c.* 1778

△ 142 Alnwick Castle. Drawing, interior, Circular Room, 1770

△ 143 Alnwick Castle. Drawing of a Gothic gateway, 1778

△ 145

◁ 144   Brislee Tower, Alnwick. Drawing, 1778

145   Brislee Tower, Alnwick, 1778–9

△ 147　Oxenfoord Castle. Garden front, 1780–2

△146　Auchincruive. Garden tower, 1778　　▽ 148　Dalquharran Castle. S. front, 1785

△ 149

149 Edinburgh, part of a perspective view of buildings, S. Bridge, 1785

△ 150 Edinburgh, design for a Triumphal Arch, c. 1785

◁ 151 The University, Edinburgh. Main
entrance, 1789–91

152 Pitfour Castle, *c.* 1790   ▷

▽ 153 Newliston. E. front, 1790–2

△ 154 Fitzroy Square, London. E. side, 1790–1800

▽ 155 Charlotte Square, Edinburgh. N. elevation, 1791

▽ 156 Trades Hall, Glassford Street,
Glasgow, 1791–9

△ 157 Design for cornice, bracket, vase,
door furniture, 1770

△ 158 Door knob and escutcheon, Dining Room, Kedleston, 1766

△ 159 Detail of chimneypiece, c. 1768,
Red Drawing Room, Syon House

△ 160 Detail of conjoined rams' heads, side table, *c.* 1765, Red Drawing Room, Syon House

161 Drawing, 1773, commode for Duke of Bolton

162 Drawing, 1774, harpsichord for Empress of Russia ▷

△ 161

the Empress of Russia

Adelphi
1774.

△ 163   Cabinet for the Duchess of Manchester by Ince and Mayhew, 1771–5

△ 164 *Ruins of the Palace of the Emperor Diocletian*, 1764. Detail from pl. 69

▽ 165 Detail of ormolu mount, Duchess of Manchester's cabinet, *c.* 1775

△ 166   Drawing, 1774, a bed for Lord
Stanley

167   State Bed, 1776–7, Osterley Park ▷

△ 168 Detail of carved sphinx, State Bed

△▽ 170–1 Chair and detail, 1764, by John Cobb for Croome Court

△ 169 Tripod stand, *c.* 1776. Osterley Park

△ 172 Candelabrum by John Carter,
1774, London hallmark

173 Monument to Lt-Col. Roger
Townshend, *c.* 1761, Westminster Abbey
▷

Design of a Monument for the late Robert Wood Esq.

Rob Adam Arch 1775.

Sculps 29 July 1773

◁ 174 Drawing, 1775, monument to Robert Wood

175 Drawing, 1780, monument to Major John André ▷

▽ 176 Detail of monument to Major John André, 1780

Sacred to the Memory

Of the most noble MARY Dutchess of MONTAGU Daughter & Coheir of IOHN Duke of MONTAGU
And Grand Daughter (by the Mother's side) of that renowned HERO Iohn Duke of MARLBOR...

This truly excellent & accomplished Lady

Exchanged this life for a better on the first of May ...

In the fifty third Year of her Age.

Her Grace had Issue by her beloved Confort GEORGE Duke of MONTAGU ...
who having had the misfortune to furvive her out of Love, Duty & Gratitude erected this MONUMENT

IOHN Marquiss of MONTHERMER, cut off in the prime of life

to the infinite regret of his noble Parents, Country & Friends.

ELIZABETH Dutchess of BUCCLEUGH her only furviving Child.

The Ladies MARY & HENRIETTA MONTAGU, who died young.

◁ 177 Monument to Mary, Duchess of
Montagu, 1775

△ 178 Boodle's Club, London. Saloon,
1775, by John Crunden

△ 179 McIntire Garden House, Danvers, Mass., 1793

▽ 180 Boscobel, Montrose, New York, 1804–7

△ 181   Willow Brook, Baltimore, Maryland. Ceiling of Oval Room, *c.* 1800

1 Binding of Robert Adam's book on Diocletian's Palace (presentation copy for George III), 1764 ▷

◁ 2 Croome Court. Tapestry Room,   △ 3 Kedleston. Saloon, 1761–2
N.W. corner, 1760–9

△ 4 Osterley Park. Drawing Room, *c.*   ▽ 5 Osterley Park. Eating Room, *c.* 1767
1773

△ 6 Osterley Park. Tapestry Room, *c.*
1773

△ 7 Osterley Park. Drawing of a firescreen, 1776

8 Osterley Park. Etruscan Dressing
Room, c. 1775–6
▷

◁ 9 Syon House. Drawing Room, 1762–4   △ 10 Syon House. Drawing Room, door to Long Gallery, c. 1766–7

△ 11 Syon House. Detail of Drawing
Room ceiling, 1764–5

▽ 12 Syon House. Long Gallery, *c.*
1763–8

△ 13 Syon House. S.W. corner, Long
Gallery

△ 14   Syon House. Detail of panel, Long   15   Syon House. Ante-Room, *c.* 1761–5▷
Gallery

◁ 16 Lansdowne House. First Drawing
Room, 1767–73

△ 17 Audley End. Great Drawing
Room, c. 1762–5

△ 18 Harewood House. Detail of Long
Gallery ceiling, c. 1768–9

△ 19   Harewood House. Detail of Long
Gallery ceiling, *c.* 1768–9

△ 20   Harewood House. Music Room, *c.*
1765–71

△ 21 Harewood House. Design for
Dressing Room ceiling, 1767

△ 22   Nostell Priory. Tapestry Room,
1767

△ 23 Nostell Priory. Saloon, *c.* 1768–76

△ 24 Nostell Priory. Top Hall, *c.* 1773–5

Cieling of a room at Mr. Montagu's House in Hill Street

△ 25   Drawing, 1766, 'Cieling of a room
at Mrs Montagu's House'

▽ 26   Drawing, *c.* 1766, 'Carpet for Mrs
Montagu'

Carpet for Mrs. Montagu —

◁ 27 Newby Hall. Library, *c.* 1769–70   △ 28 Newby Hall. Detail of Library
ceiling, *c.* 1770

△ 29 Newby Hall. Detail of Tapestry
Room ceiling, *c.* 1770

▽ 30 Newby Hall. Detail of Tapestry   31   Newby Hall. Entrance Hall, *c.* 1771 ▷
Room, *c.* 1770–5

32 Newby Hall. Design for Drawing
Room ceiling, *c.* 1770   ▷

Design of a Cieling for the Drawing Room at Newby.

Scale of   1 2 3 4 5 10   15   20   25   30 Feet

△ 33 Newby Hall. Sculpture Gallery,
1767–72

△ 34   Kenwood. Library, 1767–9

◁ 35   Saltram. Dining Room, 1768–9;
remodelled 1780–1

36 ▷

36   Painted Roundel by Zucchi, c. 1772,
originally at No. 4 Royal Terrace

△ 37   No. 6 Royal Terrace. Design for
ceiling of front Drawing Room, 1769

◁ 38　Mellerstain. Library, 1770–1　　　▽ 39　Mellerstain. Detail of centre of Library ceiling, *c.* 1770–1

△ 40　Mellerstain. Ceiling of Corner Dressing Room, *c.* 1775　　　41　Mellerstain. Drawing Room, *c.* 1778 ▷

Section of the Drawing Room Northumberl...

△ 42 Northumberland House. 'Section of the Drawing Room', *c.* 1773

43 Northumberland House. Detail of Glass Drawing Room, *c.* 1773–5 ▷

◁ 44 & ▽ 46   No. 20 St James's Square. Details of the second Drawing Room ceiling

△ 45   No. 20 St James's Square. Design for ceiling of second Drawing Room, 1772

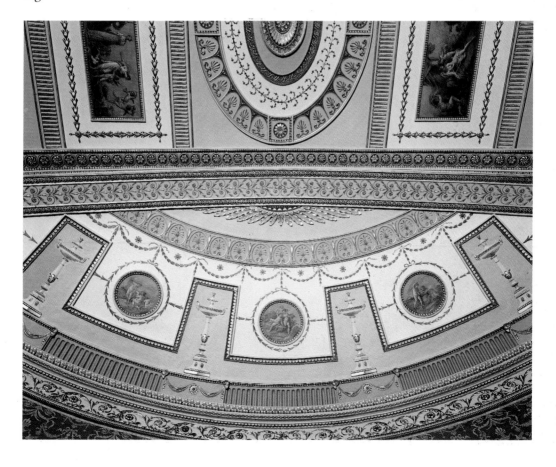

△ 47 Derby House. Drawing, 1774,
'Chimney Piece for the Bow Dressing
Room'

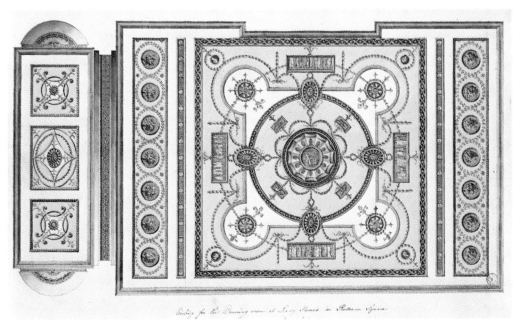

Ceiling for the Drawing room at Mrs. Hones in Portman Square

△ 48 No. 20 Portman Square. Design for Drawing Room ceiling, 1775

▽ 49 Culzean Castle. Exterior from S.W., *c.* 1777–80

◁ 50 Culzean Castle. Round Drawing
Room, *c.* 1790

△ 51 Culzean Castle. Oval Staircase,
1787

△ 52　Culzean Castle. Dining Room, c. 1780

53　Detail of recess in Princess Royal's Sitting Room, c. 1768, Harewood House, containing Chippendale commode, 1773▷

△ 54 Suite of Chippendale furniture, 1769–71, for Dining Room, Harewood House

▽ 55 Drawing of a sofa, 1764

△ 56   Design for a bed, 1776, Osterley Park

57 Design for an organ case, 1781, Cumberland House

58   Organ in Entrance Hall, Newby Hall, c. 1771   ▷

57▷

Design of an Organ Case for His Royal Highness The Dukes of Cumberland.

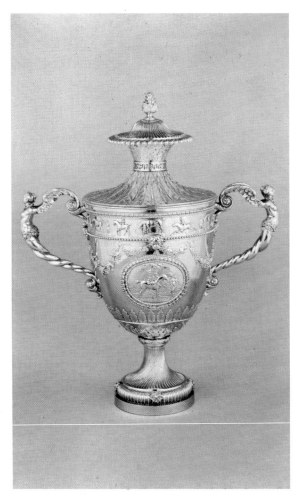

△ 60   Anglesey Cup, London, 1764

△ 59   Candlestick by John Carter, London, 1767

Appendix I

CHRONOLOGY

1689, 30 October   William Adam, Robert's father, born at Kirkcaldy (pl. 2).

1716, 30 May   William Adam married Mary Robertson (pl. 3).

1721, 5 March   John Adam, Robert's elder brother, born (pl. 4).

1728, 3 July   Robert Adam born at Kirkcaldy (pls. 1, 5).

1729   William Adam appointed Surveyor of the King's Works in Scotland.

1732, 21 July   James Adam, Robert's 'architect brother', born (pl. 6).

1734   Robert attended Edinburgh High School.

1743   Robert matriculated at Edinburgh University (then called 'College') and entered on 1 November.

1745   Robert's college career interrupted by the '45 rebellion.

1746   Robert joined John as an apprentice-assistant to his father.

1748, 24 June   William Adam died. Buried at Greyfriars' Churchyard, Edinburgh.

1750   The Adam brothers' first major commission started at Hopetoun House, near Edinburgh (pls. 21–8).

1754, October   Robert left for his Grand Tour in the entourage of Charles Hope, younger brother of the Earl of Hopetoun.

1755, 24 February   Robert arrived in Rome. (For details of the Grand Tour *see* Bibliography (Books), Fleming.)

1757   Robert travelled to Dalmatia to survey Diocletian's Palace.

1758, 17 January   Robert returned to London and set up house in Lower Grosvenor Street.

1758, 1 February   Robert admitted to membership of the Royal Society of Arts.

1760   James Adam left on his Grand Tour.

1761, July   Mary Adam, Robert and James's mother, died.

1761, November   Robert appointed 'Architect of the King's Works', jointly with William Chambers.

1761, 10 December   Robert admitted a Fellow of the Society of Antiquaries of London.

1763, October   James returned from his Grand Tour and joined Robert in London.

1764   Robert published his book *Ruins of the Palace of the Emperor Diocletian, at Spalatro, in Dalmatia* (col. pl. 1). William Adam & Company established.

1768–74   Robert Member of Parliament for Kinross-shire.

1768   James appointed 'Architect of the King's Works' when Robert relinquished the post.

1773   Robert and James published the first volume of the *Works in Architecture of Robert and James Adam* (vol. 2 1779; vol. 3 – posthumous – 1822).

1773, 25 February to 2 March   Christie's sale of the Adams' antique collections.

1792, 3 March   Robert Adam died suddenly at his home, 13 Albemarle Street, from the bursting of a blood vessel in his stomach.

1792, 10 March   Robert buried in the south transept of Westminster Abbey in the Poets' Corner.

1792, 25 June   John Adam died in Edinburgh.

1794, 20 October   James Adam died at the Albemarle Street house.

1801   Bankruptcy of William Adam & Company.

1818, 20–2 May   The Second Adam Sale by Christie's.

1821, 9 July   The Third Adam Sale by Christie's.

1822, January   William Adam, the youngest brother, died in London.

1833   Sir John Soane acquired the collection of Adam drawings.

Appendix II
BUILDINGS AND MONUMENTS BY ROBERT ADAM

(overleaf)

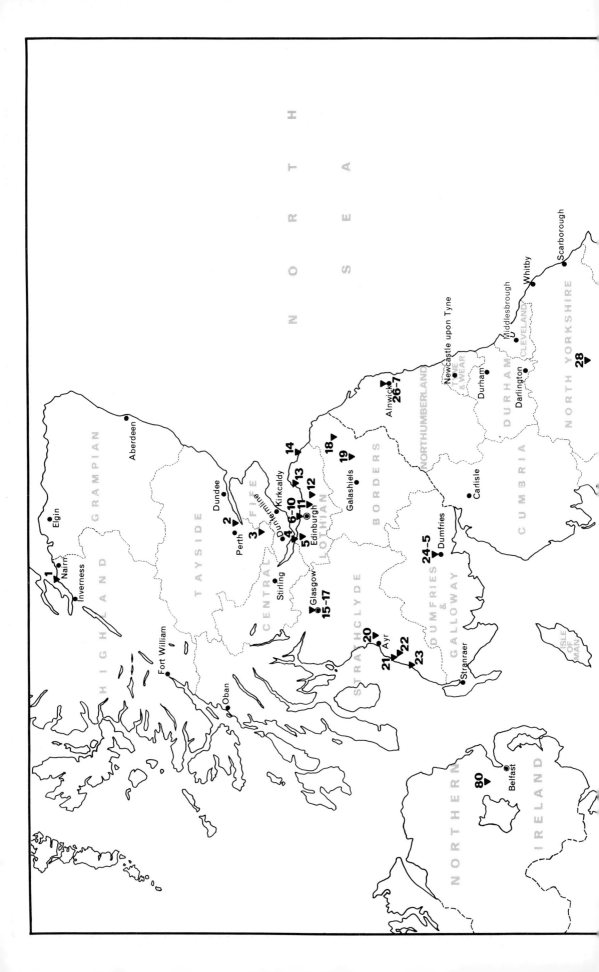

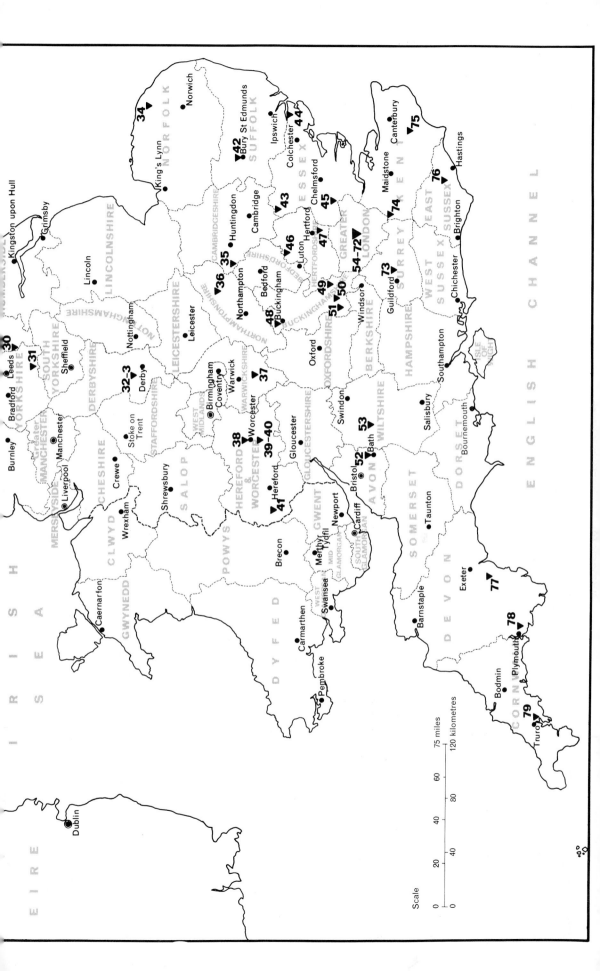

Key

The preceding map and the key below indicate those buildings and monuments that survive as examples of Adam's work at the time of writing. When a building or monument is the subject of a photograph in this book the relevant plate number is given in the key. For buildings that were not executed, or have subsequently been altered or demolished, the reader is referred to A. T. Bolton, *The Architecture of Robert and James Adam* (2 vols., 1922) and H. M. Colvin, *A Biographical Dictionary of British Architects, 1600–1840*, 2nd edn (1978).

Counties named in the key are those that existed before local-government reorganization (1974 and 1975). The relation of the buildings and monuments listed here to the new counties can be seen by reference to the map.

1 FORT GEORGE, Inverness-shire, 1752– . Fortifications for Board of Ordnance (pls. 29–30).

2 PITFOUR CASTLE, Perthshire. Castellated, *c.* 1790, for John Richardson (pl. 152).

3 COUNTY HOUSE, Kinross. South end, 1771 (at Robert Adam's expense, as the plaque thereon records).

4 HOPETOUN HOUSE, West Lothian. Continued work of William Adam: pavilions, interiors, 1751– , for 1st Earl of Hopetoun (pls. 21–8).

5 NEWLISTON, West Lothian, 1790–2, for Thomas Hog (pl. 153).

6 THE GENERAL REGISTER HOUSE, Edinburgh, 1774–92 (pls. 129–30); rear by Sir Robert Reid.

7 THE UNIVERSITY, Edinburgh, 1789–91 (pl. 151); later additions by W. H. Playfair and Sir Rowand Anderson.

8 CHARLOTTE SQUARE, Edinburgh, 1791–1807 (pl. 155).

9 NO. 7 QUEEN STREET (now Royal College of Physicians), Edinburgh, 1770–1, for Chief Baron Orde (pl. 119).

10 Monument to DAVID HUME (d. 1776), erected 1778, Old Calton churchyard, Edinburgh.

11 BRIDGE, Dalkeith, Midlothian, 1792.

12 OXENFOORD CASTLE, Midlothian. Castellated, 1780–2, for Sir John Dalrymple (pl. 147).

13 GOSFORD HOUSE, Longniddry, East Lothian, 1792–1803, for the Earl of Wemyss.

14 DUNBAR HOUSE, East Lothian. Remodelled for the Earl of Lauderdale, 1790–2.

15 ASSEMBLY ROOMS, Glasgow, 1796–8. Part of façade, alone, survives.

16 POLLOK HOUSE, Glasgow. Built house designed by William Adam, 1752, for Sir John Maxwell (pl. 31).

17 TRADES HALL, Glasgow, 1791–9 (pl. 156).

18 WEDDERBURN CASTLE, Duns, Berwickshire. Castellated, 1770, for Patrick Home (pl. 123).

19 MELLERSTAIN, Berwickshire. Castellated, interiors, 1770–8, for George

Baillie of Jerviswood (col. pls. 38–41; pls. 120–2).

20 AUCHINCRUIVE, Ayrshire. Garden tower, 1778, for Richard Oswald (pl. 146).

21 CULZEAN CASTLE, Ayrshire. Castellated, oval staircase, 1777–90, for the Earl of Cassillis (col. pls. 49–52; pls. 137–9); also farm buildings (now visitors' centre).

22 KIRKOSWALD CHURCH, Ayrshire, 1777, for the Earl of Cassillis (see Culzean Castle [21]).

23 DALQUHARRAN CASTLE, Girvan, Ayrshire. Castellated, 1785, for Thomas Kennedy (now a ruin: pl. 148).

24 DUMFRIES HOUSE, Ayrshire. Designed by John and Robert Adam, built 1754–9, for William, 5th Earl of Dumfries (pl. 32).

25 Column to memory of DUKE OF QUEENSBERRY (d. 1778), erected 1780, Market Place, Dumfries.

26 BRISLEE TOWER, Alnwick, Northumberland. Gothic folly, c. 1778–9, for 1st Duke of Northumberland (pls. 144–5).

27 HULNE PRIORY, Alnwick, Northumberland. Gothic interiors, c. 1778, for 1st Duke of Northumberland (pl. 141).

28 NEWBY HALL, Ripon, Yorkshire. Porch, wings, interiors, 1767–80, for William Weddell (col. pls. 27–33; pls. 102–6).

29 HAREWOOD HOUSE, Yorkshire, 1759–71, for Edwin Lascelles, Lord Harewood (col. pls. 18–21; pls. 93–7).

30 BYRAM HALL, Yorkshire. Library and other interiors, 1780, for Sir John Ramsden.

31 NOSTELL PRIORY, Wakefield, Yorkshire. Added wing, stables, interiors, 1766–70, for Sir Rowland Winn (col. pls. 22–4; pls. 100–1).

32 KEDLESTON HOUSE, Derbyshire. South front, interiors, bridge, fishing-house, 1760–70, for Lord Scarsdale (col. pl. 3; pls. 43–7).

33 Monument to SIR NATHANIEL CURZON (d. 1758), Kedleston church, Derbyshire; sculptor: J. M. Rysbrack.

34 GUNTON CHURCH, Norfolk, 1769, for Sir William Harbord (pl. 117).

35 KIMBOLTON CASTLE, Huntingdonshire. Gatehouse and entrance screen, 1765 (pl. 98).

36 Monument to MARY, 3rd DUCHESS OF MONTAGU (d. 1771), Warkton church, Northamptonshire; sculptor: Peter Mathias Vangelder (pl. 177).

37 COMPTON VERNEY, Warwickshire. Wings, interiors, orangery, bridge, 1761–5, for Lord Willoughby de Broke (pl. 49).

38 Monument to BISHOP JAMES JOHNSON (d. 1774), Worcester Cathedral; sculptor: Joseph Nollekens.

39 CROOME COURT, Croome d'Abitot, Worcestershire. Interiors, certain garden buildings, 1760–80, for George William, 6th Earl of Coventry (col. pl. 2; pls. 38–41).

40 CROOME CHURCH, Croome d'Abitot, Worcestershire. Fittings in Gothic style, 1763 (pl. 91).

41 MOCCAS COURT, Herefordshire, 1775–81 (built by Anthony Keck), for Sir George Cornewall.

42 THEATRE AND MARKET HALL (now Town Hall), Bury St Edmunds, Suffolk, 1775–80 (pl. 132).

43 AUDLEY END, Essex. Interiors, particularly Great Drawing Room, 1762–5, for Sir John Griffin Griffin (col. pl. 17).

44 MISTLEY CHURCH, Essex, 1776, for Richard Rigby. Demolished except for twin towers (now ruinous).

45 WEALD HALL, Essex. Interiors, 1778, for Christopher Towers.

46 HITCHIN PRIORY, Hertfordshire. South front, 1777, for John Radcliffe.

47 WORMLEYBURY, Hertfordshire. Interiors, 1777–9, for Sir Abraham Hume.

48 STOWE, Buckinghamshire. Garden front, portico, 1771– , for Earl Temple (pl. 124).

49 SHARDELOES, Buckinghamshire. Portico, interiors, stables, 1759–61, for William Drake (pls. 36–7).

50 SHAMBLES AND BUTTER MARKET, High Wycombe, Buckinghamshire, 1761 (pl. 48).

51 WEST WYCOMBE PARK, Buckinghamshire. Kitchen and stable wing, 1767–8, for Sir James Dashwood.

52 PULTENEY BRIDGE, Bath, Somerset, 1769–74, for William Pulteney (pl. 118).

53 BOWOOD HOUSE, Wiltshire. Portico, interiors, 1761–4; mausoleum, 1763; for John, Earl of Shelburne, later 1st Marquess of Lansdowne (pls. 50–5). *See also* Lansdowne House [57].

54 ADELPHI, London, begun 1772, demolished except No. 7 ADAM STREET; ceiling of No. 6 ROYAL TERRACE, re-erected at Victoria & Albert Museum (col. pl. 37); medallion from No. 4 ROYAL TERRACE (col. pl. 36; pl. 116).

55 ADMIRALTY, London. Screen wall, 1760; altered 1827 by G. L. Taylor and since restored (pl. 42).

56 ASHBURNHAM HOUSE (now No. 30), Dover Street, London, 1773–6, for Lord Ashburnham.

57 LANSDOWNE HOUSE, Berkeley Square, London, 1762, for 1st Marquess of Lansdowne. Drawing room re-created at Philadelphia Museum of Art (col. pl. 16); Dining Room at Metropolitan Museum, New York.

58 CHANDOS HOUSE, Chandos Street, London, 1770, for Duke of Chandos.

59 NO. 30 CURZON STREET, London, 1771, for Hon. H. F. Thynne.

60 FITZROY SQUARE, London, 1790–1800. South and east sides (pl. 154).

61 MANSFIELD STREET, London, 1770–5.

62 NORTHUMBERLAND HOUSE, London, 1770; demolished 1874. Glass Drawing Room re-erected at Victoria & Albert Museum (col. pls. 42–3).

63 NO. 106 PICCADILLY, London. Interiors, 1765–6, for 6th Earl of Coventry.

64 NO. 20 PORTMAN SQUARE, London (Home House, now Courtauld Institute of Fine Art, University of London), 1775–7 (pls. 133–6).

65 ROYAL SOCIETY OF ARTS, John Street, London, 1772–4 (pls. 112–13).

66 No. 20 St James's Square, London, 1772–4, for Sir Watkin Williams-Wynn (col. pls. 44–6; pls. 125–6).

67 No. 29 Sackville Street, London. Ceiling, 1770, for John Parker of Saltram.

68 Westminster Abbey, London: monuments to Major John André (d. 1780), sculptor Peter Mathias Vangelder (pls. 175–6); Mary Hope (d. 1767), sculptor not known; Elizabeth, Duchess of Northumberland (d. 1776), sculptor Nicholas Read; James Thomson (d. 1748), sculptor Michael Spang, erected 1762; Lt-Col. Roger Townshend (d. 1759), sculptors Thomas Carter and John Eckstein (pl. 173).

69 Kenwood House, Hampstead, Middlesex. Library, portico, 1767–9, for 1st Earl of Mansfield (col. pl. 34; pls. 107, 109–10).

70 Osterley House, Middlesex, 1761–80, for Robert Child (col. pls. 4–8; pls. 56–78).

71 Syon House, Middlesex. Remodelled interior (col. pls. 9–15; pls. 79–86), 1762–9, for 1st Duke of Northumberland; entrance screen, 1773 (pl. 87).

72 Monument to Robert Child (d. 1782), Heston church, Middlesex. Sculptor Peter Mathias Vangelder.

73 Hatchlands, Surrey. Interiors, 1758– 61, for Admiral the Hon. Edward Boscawen (pls. 33–5).

74 Brasted House, Kent, 1784–5, for Dr John Turton.

75 Mersham Le Hatch, Kent. House and interiors, 1762–5, for Sir Edward Knatchbull (pls. 89–90).

76 Ashburnham Place, Sussex. Entrance lodges, 1785, for Earl of Ashburnham.

77 Ugbrooke Park, Devon. South and west fronts, 1764–8, and some interior work, 1766–71, for Lord Clifford (pl. 92).

78 Saltram, Devon. Interior decorations, 1768–9, for John Parker – later to become Lord Boringdon (col. pl. 35; pl. 111).

79 Monument to Admiral, The Hon. Edward Boscawen (d. 1761), church (St Michael) at St Michael Penkevil, Cornwall; sculptor: J. M. Rysbrack.

80 Castle Upton, Co. Antrim, Ireland. Castellated additions, 1788, for Lord Templetown.

81 Headfort, Co. Meath, Ireland, 1770, for 1st Lord Bective. Designed by Adam but erected with some alterations to his plans and under other supervision.

INDEX